25 KITES THAT FLY

THE GREAT INTEREST OF BOYS IN KITES AND KITE FLYING IS QUITE EVIDENT FROM THE ABOVE, SHOWING A KITE-FLYING CONTEST HELD AT ORANGE, N. J., IN 1928
(Wide World Photos)

25 KITES THAT FLY

LESLIE L. HUNT

DOVER PUBLICATIONS, INC.
NEW YORK

This Dover edition, first published in 1971, is
an unabridged and unaltered republication of the
work originally published by The Bruce Publishing
Company in 1929.

International Standard Book Number: 0-486-22550-X
Library of Congress Catalog Card Number: 74-140229

Manufactured in the United States of America
Dover Publications, Inc.
180 Varick Street
New York, N. Y. 10014

To

My Children

Whose assistance and enthusiasm have rendered the writing of this book a pleasure.

PREFACE

Some time ago, I was called on to instruct a number of young women in kitemaking, who, in turn, were to act as instructors in summer church schools. This book has been the outgrowth of my lecture-demonstrations.

There are many excellent magazine articles and a few good books on kitemaking; but the articles are, for the most part, hard to find except in the larger libraries, and the books call for materials not likely to be had outside of manual-training supply houses or large lumber yards.

Since only the commonest materials are required in making the kites herein described, it is felt that this book is not duplicating the efforts of others. It is hoped that this effort will find favor with the teachers in public and special schools, with playground instructors, and in particular with the boys and girls themselves.

L. L. H.

Harvey, Illinois,
April 25, 1929

TABLE OF CONTENTS

INTRODUCTION

In preparing this book of kites, I have tried to make the directions as complete as possible without needless repetition. More details are given in the first group than in the others. After a successful two-stick kite has been made and flown, attention having been given to the lashing together of sticks, wrapping of stick ends, papering, etc., further kite-making will resolve itself into following the patterns.

There may be better ways of lashing and framing kites than those given here, and, no doubt, there may be objections raised to making large kites by these methods. But this book was designed as a guide to the making and flying of moderate-sized kites, and it is not planned to treat of knots and lashings, nor to go deeply into the professional aspects of kitemaking. On the contrary, everything else is kept subordinate to the idea of presenting such directions for making kites that fly as can be carried out, without previous kitemaking experience, in almost any home.

I have rarely indicated the thickness of the sticks. Unless specified, the thickness is to be 3/16 inch which is about the thickness one is able to get from the material described. If one wishes to make a kite twice as large, it will be better to double the thickness of the stick instead of doubling the width. Of course, other material will have to be used, or the sticks built up as described in Chapter VII.

I have allowed a liberal amount of the stick to project beyond the margins of the kites. Experience has taught me that a broken stick is easier to replace than it is to make extensive repairs in the paper or to repair both stick and paper. The projecting stick ends save the paper, and do not render the sticks any more likely to break.

I have recommended slitting the ends of the sticks with a thin saw to receive the framing string. If no thin saw is at hand, the sticks may be notched with a sharp knife and lashed in place as shown in Figure 2.

Some kites cannot be framed entirely with framing string without using too many sticks. I reduce the number of sticks to the minimum, and use a dark-colored framing string, letting it go where it will. A dark-colored string is not noticed when the kite is flying. If any sticks show, a little ink and chalk will tone the color of the wood to a tint that will be little noticed. Of course, there will be places in the kite that will need stiffening. I use trough-shaped papers like that shown in the central sketch in Figure 4 for such stiffening, and if such support is not easily fitted, I use shavings or slivers of wood glued to the paper as shown in the lower sketch of the same figure. When the papers or slivers are dried under moderate pressure, that part of the kite becomes quite rigid, and but little is added to the weight.

Many methods of tying, stiffening, and trimming will suggest themselves to the kitemaker after the work is begun.

25 KITES THAT FLY

CHAPTER I

KITEMAKING IN GENERAL

Is there anyone who has not felt the desire to fly a kite and feel it tug away at its string like a living thing? The joy of kiteflying is greatly increased when we make our own kites and have the satisfaction of seeing them rise gracefully on the lightest breeze, or soar swiftly to a great height with a stronger wind and cut capers in a bright blue sky.

Many boys and girls do not make their own kites for fear they will not fly, but it is just as easy to make a kite that will fly as it is to make one that will not. In fact, most of the nonfliers can be made to fly with just a few minutes' thoughtful work. If you have a kite that does not fly well, do not throw it away, but read the description of the kite most like it in this book and see whether you cannot correct its faults. If you do not already have a kite, you will be able to make any number of satisfactory fliers by following the directions in Chapters II, III, and IV.

The author has made all the kites described in this book and rated them as excellent, good, moderate, and fair fliers. Even the fair fliers may be put up in a moderate breeze without a great amount of running, and fly high enough to show their decorative character to the best advantage. The kites rated as excellent, fly in the lightest breezes, and with a small, smooth string will climb quickly to a great height. It is impossible to say how high any of the kites will fly, as only 1,000 feet of string was used while testing them. Several of the kites have been at the end of the string pulling for more, and flying at an angle that showed them to be several hundred feet above the ground.

Sometimes it happens that a good opportunity comes to fly a kite, but there is no time for experimenting. What is needed then is a kite that is sure to fly. This book describes various types of kites that are sure to fly and that can be made with common materials and gives directions for making them. I have had such splendid results with sticks cut

Kites, varying in kind and size, but each the proud achievement of the boys who participated in the kiteflying contest held at Orange, N. J.
(Wide World Photos)

from the boards of orange crates that I have decided to pass the good news on to others.

We may consider kites as either high-flying or decorative. Common flat kites, bow kites, and box kites are suitable for high flights, while the figure kites are designed more for decoration. There is no object in making a high-flying kite decorative since brilliant color combinations lose much of their near-at-hand vividness when high in the air. In making a high-flying kite, it is better to spend a little extra effort on neatness and on cutting down weight than on decorations. While it is best to keep the decorative kites as light as possible, still a little added weight for the sake of stiffness is not as objectionable as it would be in the case of the high fliers.

THE QUESTION OF SIZE

The author has made kites of all sizes; from the tiniest, made of broom straws and thin tissue paper and flown with No. 100 thread, to huge affairs flown with braided clothes lines that were real problems to make and store. If one increases the size of a kite indefinitely, the extra stiffness needed for the large kite makes the weight greater in proportion to its size, and a point is soon reached where the weight begins to increase faster than the lifting power. On the other hand, if one makes a kite very small, it may be too flimsy to fly well. In a word, large kites are often too heavy, and small kites too frail to give the best results. A length of 20 to 40 inches will be satisfactory. If you need more pull or lifting power, use two or more kites on the same string some distance apart.

KINDS OF KITES

Considering the kinds of kites from the way they are constructed, there are those having one plane surface, those having a surface or surfaces not in the same plane, and combinations of the two kinds.

The plane-surface kites must have a tail or suitable substitute, which does not disfigure the kite, if it is properly made. A pretty tail is as much an adornment to a kite as a pretty tail is to a bird.

Kites having surfaces not in one plane do not need tails, although tails and pennants may be attached after a little experimenting. As a rule, it is better to carry the decorations on a rigging attached to the string some distance below the kites as described in Chapter VI.

Combination kites require no tails, if the plane surfaces are of equal or less area than the curved or oblique surfaces.

MATERIALS AND TOOLS

Fruit crates, especially orange and lemon crates that are made of sawed boards, provide excellent material for kite sticks. The crates made of veneering are not suitable. Veneer does not show the rough surface left by the saw, and may be easily distinguished by its tendency to split and curl. An ordinary crate has eight boards about 5 inches wide, 26 inches long and a trifle less than a quarter of an inch thick. Even if one doesn't get the two top boards there is enough material to get two dozen full-length sticks, if one uses care in cutting them out. I have found it better to cut the sticks with a knife than to use a saw. Study the direction of the grain in the board from which you are cutting the sticks, and lay a straight board along the grain and cut along the edge of the board with two or three firm strokes of the knife. The stick may then be detached with the fingers and will require very little dressing to make it ready for use. If the sticks are first marked out with a pencil, time will be saved and disappointment may be avoided.

If quiet flying is desired, crêpe paper is superior to smooth paper in spite of its extra weight. It may be had in many colors and in a large number of brilliant patterns. When one wants to make a kite that will dance or perform antics, smooth or even glazed paper seems better. For all ordinary flying, plain tissue paper is excellent.

Thin wrapping paper serves well for box kites, since considerable strain comes on the paper and thin or crêpe papers would have to be reënforced. Crêpe paper is difficult to paste, but thin paste and quick work will solve the difficulty. Glue is better than paste.

Liquid glue and prepared paste are preferred on account of their convenience and keeping properties, but, if neither is at hand, a thoroughly cooked flour paste may be used. The tapioca paste described in Chapter VII is a little troublesome to make, but it keeps well and has wonderful sticking qualities.

Glue is preferable for work with the sticks. It gives a stiffness to the joints that is desirable. A string dipped in rather hot paste and wrapped around the sticks where they cross will make a strong joint, although, with a little help, one can do nearly as well with string alone. If a wire is used to fasten sticks together, it will be well to shape the wire to the sticks before twisting it tight. By shaping the wire first, cutting the sticks is avoided. Some kitemakers fasten their sticks together with brads. Select a brad to correspond to the size of the stick used; those obtained from cigar boxes are about the right size for the kites here described. One brad with a few turns of string will make a stronger joint than two or more brads alone.

In applying decorations, such as those cut out of paper napkins and the like, do not use too much paste. No matter if the decorations flutter a little, this fluttering usually makes them all the more attractive while in the air. Decorate boldly. Colors that appear startling close up are greatly modified when flying. Contrasts may be kept by running a bold dark band between the colors, or by selecting the colors desired, and then using the dark color of the selection and a subdued lighter color. For example, a blue-and-orange combination has strong contrast near at hand, but when high in the air, the colors merge toward a gray. The contrast may be revived by running a black stripe between the colors, or by using an ocher instead of a bright yellow.

Few tools are required. A good knife, with a means of keeping it sharp, a pencil, a rule, a large darning needle, and a hammer are all that are actually needed. If a small plane is handy, it will be found very useful. A thin-blade saw, such as a hack saw or coping saw may be used to slit the ends of the sticks, but if no saw of this kind may be had, the stick ends may be notched as described in the Introduction and as shown in Figure 2.

The materials other than sticks and paper that are needed are easily obtained. Some string will be needed for tying and framing, which may be the same kind as that selected for flying the kite. A tube or liquid glue, a bottle of paste with brush, a few ¼-inch rubber bands, about 20 feet of No. 18 covered iron wire, and paper festooning makes up the list. The wire may not be needed in the kite you wish to build, and material other than festooning may be used for the tail.

Before starting to build any kite, it will be well to read the Introduction and the directions for making the two-stick kite. Many small and essential details are given in the suggestions and directions just mentioned that will not be repeated in the descriptions of the other kites. Should you have trouble in getting your kite to fly, make sure you have followed the directions carefully and study the suggestions given in Chapter V.

CHAPTER II

PLANE-SURFACE KITES

No. 1. A TWO-STICK KITE

Prepare two sticks ⅜ by ¼ by 26 inches and trim them
until they are about ¼ inch wide and quite straight. Plane
or scrape the sides very lightly, just enough to make them
clean. Take the straighter stick and trim each end to good
solid wood, bringing the length to exactly 26 inches. Mark
the edges ½ inch from each end, and saw a narrow slit

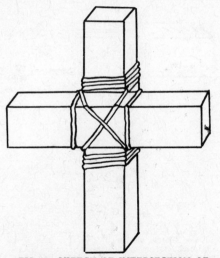

FIG. 1. SKETCH OF INTERSECTION OF
STICKS, SHOWING METHOD OF WRAPPING
Tie on other side with a knot like that shown in
Fig. 2.

parallel to the flat sides down to the mark, or notch the ends
as shown in Figure 2. This stick is the spine.

Prepare the other stick in the same manner, only making
the total length 22 inches. This stick is for the cross.

From the end of the spine selected for the top, mark 7
and 7¼ inches. From each end of the cross, measure 10⅞

inches and mark all around. These marks designate the place
where the sticks will intersect.

Apply a thin coat of glue and place the sticks in position.
Square the intersection with one of the end boards of the
crate, a book or other suitable object. Tie the sticks in place
as shown in Figure 1, using care to keep them at right angles
and in the proper position.

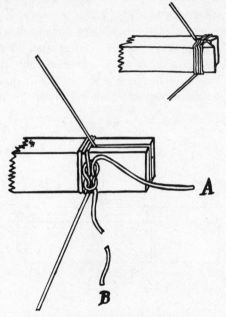

FIG. 2. END OF STICK, SHOWING METHOD OF FIRST
PART OF WRAPPING
After knot is tightened, lay end of string A along stick
and wrap with B about four turns, securing the framing
string in the slit as shown in Fig. 3. The small sketch
shows the stick end notched instead of slit. Either method
works very well and allows new sticks to be put in without
disturbing the rest of the kite.

Cut four pieces of string 8 inches long and start wrapping
the ends of the sticks as shown in Figure 2. Wrap twice
around just behind the mark, tie snugly and leave the ends
free. Do not wrap too hard. To break a string while wrapping is almost sure to snap a stick.

Now take the ball of string, tie a knot about 4 inches from
the end, and frame the kite by slipping the string into the

slits or notches. Start at the top of the spine. The knot keeps the string from pulling through until you are ready to tie it to the other end of the framing string. Draw the string taut but not tight enough to bend the sticks. Tie to the free end at the top, and make final adjustments by squaring and measuring carefully.

Finish the ends of the sticks outside the framing string as shown in Figure 3, and clip off all loose ends.

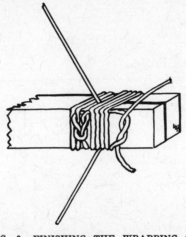

FIG. 3. FINISHING THE WRAPPING OF
THE STICK END
The first half of the knot is tied. Study
Fig. 2 to see how the second half is tied.

Open a roll of crêpe paper on a smooth surface and straighten out the wrinkles caused by the folds, being careful not to stretch the crêpe. If there is a right side to the paper, it should be placed down. Hold the paper in place with books or other convenient objects, and place the kite frame, spine side down, on the paper so the ridges of the crêpe run the long way of the frame. Bring the top of the spine even with one margin of the paper. Cut the paper larger than the kite so a hem about ¾ of an inch deep may be turned over the framing string. The triangular pieces left from the sides will be enough to make the splice at the bottom. Apply paste freely ½ inch wide to the bottom margin, and lay the splice on at once patting the paper together with the fingers. Keep the hands clean. There is nothing more annoying than to have bits of trash sticking to the fingers when one is working with string and paper.

Clip the margin carefully on each side of the sticks as far in as the framing string, and crease the paper so it will fold over readily without pulling the string out of place. Clip the

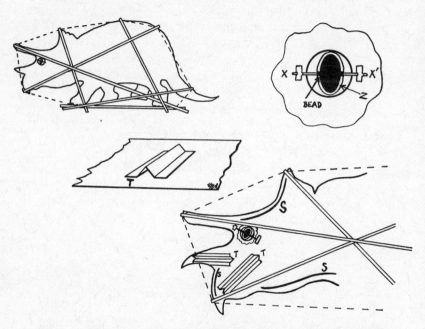

FIG. 4. METHOD OF STRENGTHENING AN IRREGULAR-FIGURE KITE
A sketch of a dinosaur, or ancient lizardlike animal, is shown in the upper left with sticks in place. The framing string is shown as a dotted line. The upper right shows the construction of a blinking eye. The black part of the drawing represents the pupil of the eye mounted on a short wire X-X'. There is a space cut out of the iris of the eye Z, so the pupil will spin with the wind. The rest of the iris is made of greased paper. The central sketch shows a trough-shaped piece of paper glued to the back of the kite surface to give it stiffness. The lower right sketch is the head of the monster showing the reënforcements just described at T, and also slivers or shavings glued on at S. This kite will require a tail. Perhaps a better way of framing can be worked out. A discussion of reënforcements is given in the Introduction.

paper so none will be pasted to the sticks and paste into place. Go right around the kite, and when all sides are pasted, set away in a warm dry place until dry. Then turn the kite over and finish the paper near the ends of the sticks by folding and pasting.

The bridle or bellyband is to be attached to the paper side of the kite. Pull the stretch out of about 8 feet of string, thread it singly on the needle, and run it under the wrapping at the upper end of the spine starting from the top. Pull the string through until about a foot remains. Run the needle under the wrapping at the lower end of the spine, starting from the top of the wrapping, and pull through so a loop about a yard long will be formed. Cut this loop about 8 inches from the bottom of the kite, and tie the short end into a $\frac{1}{4}$-inch rubber band. Pull the string so there is exactly 5 inches between the rubber band and the place where the string touches the kite. Secure the lower end with two half hitches and let the excess string hang free. Tie a knot in the other string about 8 inches from the end. Tie into the rubber band so the knot will be about two inches above the rubber. Adjust the loop thus formed to exactly 31 inches. Secure the top with two half hitches, leaving enough string hanging free for further adjustments. Bring up the string that is below the kite, and tie it above the knot so the rubber band can stretch about 4 inches before the string checks its extension. Do not pull too hard on the kite in making these adjustments, as a broken stick is sure to result.

The object of this kind of bridle is to prevent sudden gusts of wind from tearing the kite or making it dart violently. It also allows the kite to fly in various velocities of wind without adjustment and at a slightly higher angle than without it.

Attaching the horizontal string requires some patience. You should still have the needle threaded, so proceed as you did for the vertical string, only do not use the elastic arrangement. Keeping the kite flat, bridle side up, draw up the vertical bridle by means of a wire hook so the vertex of the angle formed will be exactly over the spine at a point 5 inches from the top framing string. Remember the rubber will stretch some, so do not draw tighter than necessary to give a feeling of firmness. Run the horizontal string through the hook, and pull taut. Tie a tow string or leader at this place crisscross through the intersection of the bridle. Secure

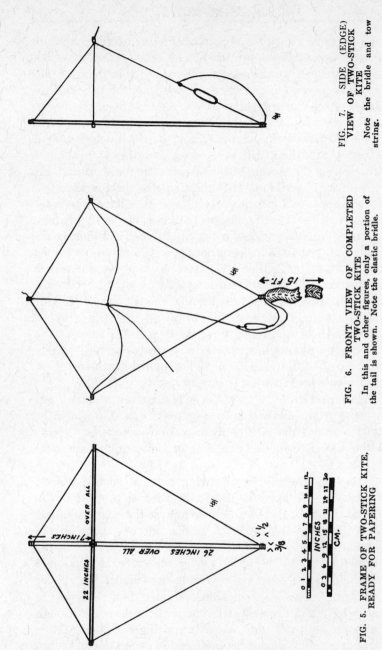

FIG. 7. SIDE (EDGE) VIEW OF TWO-STICK KITE
Note the bridle and tow string.

FIG. 6. FRONT VIEW OF COMPLETED TWO-STICK KITE
In this and other figures, only a portion of the tail is shown. Note the elastic bridle.

15 FT.

FIG. 5. FRAME OF TWO-STICK KITE, READY FOR PAPERING

7 INCHES OVER ALL

26 INCHES OVER ALL

22 INCHES

1/2

3/8

0 1 2 3 4 5 6 7 8 9 10 11
INCHES
0 3 6 9 12 15 18 21 24 27 30
CM.

with a drop of glue. Fix the ends of the horizontal string to the cross strick with two half stitches, leaving enough string at each side for further adjustments.

While the bridle described may be criticised by professional kitemakers, it is satisfactory, easy to adjust, and strong enough for the kites herein described.

Make the tail either of scraps of paper tied to a strong string at intervals of a foot, or use festoon decorations. The tail for the above kite consisted of 15 feet of 1½-inch flat festoon tied on singly. Remember a tail is not for weight as much as it is for air resistance. A string and a stone will not keep a kite as steady as a bushy or fuzzy tail of much less weight.

Attach the tail with string and glue to the lower end of the spine on the stick side of the kite. When dry, the kite is ready for use.

The dimensions and weight of the kite just described, without tail, were as follows:

Length, 25 inches; width, 21½ inches; area, 268 square inches or 1.86 square feet; weight, .88 ounces. Rating is found by dividing the number representing the weight by the number representing the square feet. In this case, .88 ÷ 1.86 = .47. The rating is therefore .47 ounce per square foot.

There is no reason why the rating of a kite should be computed unless one cares to take up the kitemaking pastime as a hobby. In that case, it is well to have a means whereby one kite may be compared with another. Since the flying power often depends on the surface and weight alone, the weight per square foot gives a ready means of comparison. Other things affecting the flying power of a kite are discussed in Chapter V.

The ratings of nearly all the kites in this book are given. The weight of the tail is not included, as the wind will support the weight of the tail, if the kite and the tail are properly made.

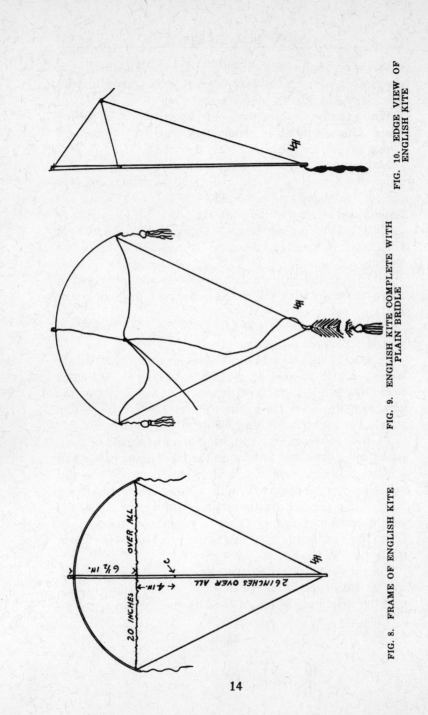

FIG. 10. EDGE VIEW OF ENGLISH KITE

FIG. 9. ENGLISH KITE COMPLETE WITH PLAIN BRIDLE

FIG. 8. FRAME OF ENGLISH KITE

14

No. 2. ENGLISH KITE

The English Kite is a modification of the Two-Stick Kite. It is usually made like the Two-Stick Kite with an arched top made of a strip of rattan or bamboo. A little care will enable one to dispense with the cross stick and to use a strip from an orange crate for the arch. Prepare the spine in the manner described for No. 1, bringing the length to 26 inches. Slit the bottom end half an inch or notch deeply. The top end need not be slit. Prepare another stick from light-colored wood, making it ⅜ by ⅛ by 26 inches. Slit the ends, but this time the slit is to run parallel to the edges.

On a sheet of paper about 1 by 2 feet, crease a line the long way about 4 inches from the bottom. Bring the two ends of this crease together and form a new crease in the middle of the first and at right angles to it. Unfold the paper and fasten it to a board or wall where you may drive nails.

From a center, 4 inches below the intersection of the creases, strike an arc of a circle having a radius of 10½ inches, as large as the paper will permit. Drive nails part way in about 2 inches apart, beginning at the top of the arch and following the curved line closely. This is the pattern or template for bending the arch stick. It will be well to keep it, as you may have occasion to use it for other kites. Tie the middle of a 3-foot string to the top nail.

See that the arch stick is of uniform thickness and mark its center. When everything is ready, pour hot water on the stick, pouring slowly back and forth from end to end until the stick seems quite soft. Tie the center of the stick to the top nail, and lash it, flat side to the nails. Proceed carefully. If the stick seems too stiff, tuck a cloth around it and pour on hot water. When the stick is shaped, tie it in place.

The stick may be bent on the outside or on the inside of the arch. If the stick is of the thickness mentioned, there will be but little difference in the width of the kite; but I find it a little easier to bend the stick on the outside of the arch.

Remove the top nail and lay the spine along the short crease of the pattern allowing the top to lap over the arch stick half an inch. Make sure that the slit in the other end is properly placed, then glue and tie as shown in Figure 1. Start wrapping the ends as shown in Figure 2.

Tie the middle of a 2-foot string around the spine just over the intersection of the creases and run the strings through the slits of the arch so as to form a cross string instead of a cross stick. Adjust the frame by the eye and by measuring. Fasten the cross strings, letting the ends hang free. Connect the ends of the arch and the bottom of the spine with a framing string. It will be well to fasten the framing string above the cross strings. Finish wrapping the ends (Fig. 3) still leaving the ends of the cross strings free.

Let the frame dry before removing from the pattern. Paper the kite, spine next to the paper, pasting the paper to the arch stick and also lapping it a little. Make two tassels of tissue paper about 4 inches in length and suspend them about half their length by means of the ends of the cross string. Clip off all loose ends and let the kite dry.

Attach the bridle as directed for the two-stick kite (No. 1) only fix the towing point about 5 inches from the top. For a 26-inch kite, the vertical loop should be 28½ inches when finished.

Complete the kite with a tail made of 18 feet of 1½-inch paper festooning, or with a tail made of scraps of light fluffy paper.

A kite made according to the above specifications rated .54 ounce per square foot, inclusive of tassels, but exclusive of tail. It was not as rigid as the two-stick kite, but it was a very satisfactory flier and a great favorite with older people who had likely flown kites of this kind when they were young.

No. 3. A THREE-STICK KITE

Prepare two sticks ¼ inch wide and 26 inches long, and a third stick the same width and 22 inches long. Slit or notch all ends and start wrapping. Cross the long sticks forming a narrow "X" making the distance from the shorter end of the "X" to the center of the intersection 9½ inches. Lay the sticks in this position on a table with the shorter end of the

"X" toward you. Have the ends of the sticks flush with the edge of the table. Lay on the short stick parallel to the edge of the table so its center falls over the center of the intersection of the legs of the "X." Without disturbing, apply glue and tie snugly.

Now spread the short ends of the "X" so the sticks will be 8 inches apart at the top, from center to center. This spreading will tighten the joint. Keep the short stick parallel to the edge of the table, lay books on the frame to hold it in position, and frame the kite. Adjust to the dimensions shown in Figure 11, this time measuring along the framing string between the sticks.

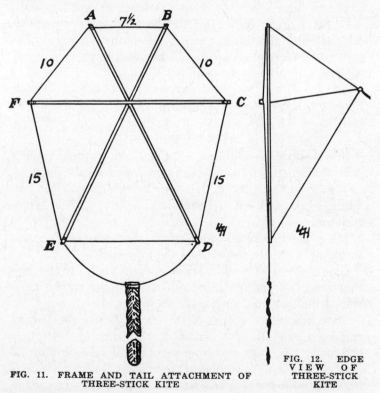

FIG. 11.   FRAME AND TAIL ATTACHMENT OF
THREE-STICK KITE

FIG. 12.   EDGE
VIEW   OF
THREE-STICK
KITE

Some kitemakers prefer to lay the cross stick a little above or below the intersection of the long sticks. This plan is a good one for large kites, but it is hardly necessary for one of this size.

Finish the wrapping of the stick ends, paper the kite, and let it dry.

It is not advisable to use an elastic bridle on these kites, as two rubber bands would be required and it is difficult to get them to pull together. The loops A to D, and B to E are 33 inches long when finished. The horizontal loop is about 30 inches in length. For attaching the bridle, follow the directions given for kite No. 1. Let the towing point lie in the center line of the kite about 10 inches from its surface and over a point about 6¾ inches from the top.

The tail may be double, a piece fastened to each leg of the "X," but I prefer connecting the legs with a loop of string and fastening the tail to the middle of the loop. This plan throws the movements of the tail farther from the center of the kite and makes it fly steadier.

The above kite rated .47 ounce per square foot. It had, therefore, the same rating as the two-stick kite, and was fully as good a flier.

No. 4. A Six-Point Star

Select a straight strip that will finish to a width of ¼ inch and to a length of 26 inches. Prepare two sticks about ¼ inch wide and 22¾ inches long. Mark the long stick 6¾ and 7 inches from each end and the short sticks 11½ inches from each end.

Slit or notch the ends of the sticks, cutting the ends of the short sticks a little deeper than the long stick.

Glue and wrap the short sticks at right angles to the long one where marked, putting both short sticks on the same side of the long one. Square the intersections.

Start wrapping the ends of the sticks. Frame the kite by running a string from one end of a short stick to the farther end of the long stick and from there to the other end of the same short stick. An equilateral triangle will be formed having a stick for one side and strings for the other. Proceed in the same manner with the other short stick, adjusting carefully. The star outline is now plainly seen. Tie and glue the intersection of the framing strings, and glue the framing strings to the sticks where they cross. If a circle is desired to surround the star, see the note at the end of this description. If the kite is to fly as a star only, finish wrapping the ends of the sticks.

Paper the kite as usual, only this time put the cross sticks next to the paper. If it is desired to use different colors, the center should be papered first, pasting the paper on the cross sticks only and allowing plenty to lap over the strings. Lay

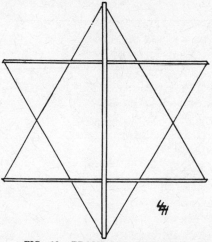

FIG. 13. FRAME OF SIX-POINT STAR

the kite paper side uppermost and paste the points on the center paper true to pattern. Turn the kite over and finish as usual. Be sure to give the kite time to dry.

The long bridle is attached to the spine, and the short bridle to the upper cross stick. An elastic bridle may be used. The towing point should be directly over the intersection of the sticks about 10 inches from the surface of the kite.

About 20 feet of 1½-inch paper festoon will be needed for a tail. The Six-Point Star Kite rated .83 ounce per square foot. It was a good flier.

NOTE: Some kitemakers like a circle around their star kites. It adds much to the beauty of the kite, and if carefully made, it need not alter the kite's rating or flying power very much. Bend a wire into a circle large enough to fit into the slits at the ends of the sticks. Fit it in position before the final wrapping of the sticks. Do not use too large a wire or too much force as the sticks are likely to split. No. 18 covered wire is large enough. Iron wire is superior to copper. Join the ends of the wire neatly and wrap the stick ends.

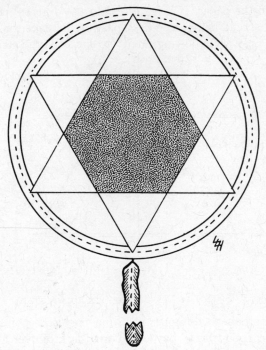

FIG. 14.   SIX-POINT STAR WITH CIRCLE
The position of the wire is shown by the dotted line.
See directions for attaching bridle.

Whip festoon along the wire with needle and thread starting at the bottom of the spine. Have the wire behind the festoon when the surface of the kite is toward you. The tail will have to be lengthened about 6 feet when the circle is added.

No. 5.   A FIVE-POINT STAR

Observe the same directions for the preparation of sticks as already given. The sticks for the Five-Point Star should be three in number, each ⅜ by 26 inches and the usual thick-

ness to be had from the orange-crate boards. Select the two
sticks that are most nearly alike for the legs of the star.
Continue the slit at one end of each of the legs for about ¾
inch and saw out so these ends will be half the usual thickness. Apply glue to the sawed surfaces and wrap together
forming a letter "V."

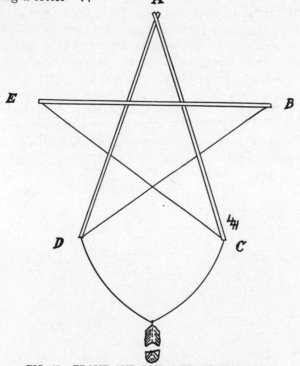

FIG. 15. FRAME AND TAIL ATTACHMENT FOR
FIVE-POINT STAR

Measure along the legs of the "V" 16 inches and mark.
Measure and mark 9½ inches from each end of the other
stick. Place the ends of the legs at the edge of a table as
described for the Six-Point Star, and lay the cross stick at
the places marked. Spread the legs to 16 inches, measuring
center to center. Adjust carefully so the distances AB, BC,
CD, DE, EA are equal. (See Fig. 15.) When the adjustments are made, glue and tie, then start wrapping the stick
ends.

Frame the kite by running strings from the ends of the legs to the farther ends of the cross stick. Glue the framing string to the legs where it crosses over.

Paper the kite and let it dry. If a circle is desired, it should be added at this time. If not, finish wrapping the sticks and snip off loose ends.

The kite is to be flown stick point uppermost. Make a bridle of two loops running from the top point to the legs. The tow string is to be tied around the two loops so the towing point will be somewhat above the center point of the cross stick about 10 inches from the kite.

About 18 feet of 1½-inch festoon will be needed for the tail. It should be attached to a loop hung from the legs of the star.

The five-point star kite, without circle, rated .9 ounce per square foot. It was a good flier.

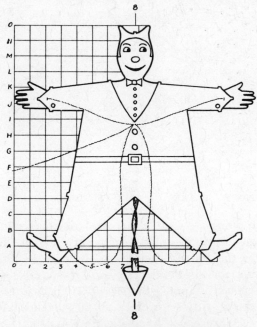

FIG. 16.   THE IMP KITE COMPLETE
The squares are 2 inches square, and are to be used in drawing the outline as described in the directions.

No. 6. The Imp

The construction of the Imp may be understood best from the figures. The same treatment of the sticks, framing strings, and paper as given heretofore should be followed. The sticks need not be wider than 3/16 of an inch.

It is first necessary to form a pattern. Select a sheet of plain paper about 2 by 3 feet and fold a crease the long way through the center. Rule one side lightly in 2-inch squares and copy the Imp outline from Figure 16. The kite is the same shape right and left, so it will be necessary to draw only one side. Hold the drawn side against a window, and trace the other half of the figure. Unfold the pattern and cut close to the outline.

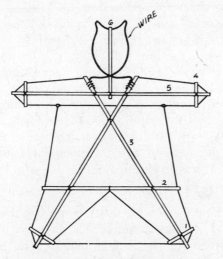

FIG. 17. FRAME OF IMP KITE
Except the wire forming the head, notice all the framing may be easily done with string.

The sticks need not be more than 3/16 inch wide, but they should be reasonably straight and pliant. Lay the sticks on the pattern to conform, but do not vary too much from the suggestions or the balance will be hard to find.

Frame the kite with string; paper as usual with appropriate colors. The head should be framed with wire and the horns supported with slivers glued on. The introduction and

Figure 4 give suggestions for stiffening parts of the kite that are flimsy.

Draw the features boldly. Cut out the eyes, and glue waxed paper over the holes on the back of the kite. Replace the iris and pupils on the waxed paper and you will have a pair of eyes well suited to any Imp. The hands and feet may now be added. These are to be cut from stiff paper, tinted, and reënforced by slivers or trough-shape papers, as shown in Figure 4.

Run a loop from one wrist to the other, and another loop from one ankle to the other. The first loop should be about 24 inches when finished and the other loop about 44 inches. The towing point will be along the line joining the centers of the wrists about 5½ inches from the kite.

About 15 feet of 1½-inch festoon will be needed for a tail. Tie the tail midway between the feet with a taut string; if this is neglected, the Imp will oscillate in the air and prove a poor flier. Complete the tail with a spearhead made of a cone of thin cardboard covered with red paper. Glue the tail deep in the cone and center it at the top by means of cross strings. The cone should be about 5 inches long and about 4 inches in diameter. Do not make it too heavy.

A kite made by the above directions, rated .61 ounce per square foot. It was an excellent flier.

No. 7.   GIRL WITH SKIPPING ROPE

The suggestions given for the Imp apply to this kite, since the right and left sides are alike. The sticks should be about 3/16 inch wide and the lengths indicated in the sketches. Instead of framing the kite with string and wire, glue the pattern to the sticks. Now glue the paper representing the clothing to the face of the kite folding over the edges about an inch. The skirt should be cut full and fixed in place first. A study of shop windows will give suggestions for color and decoration. An orange dress with green and purple trimmings looks well when flying, although one would hardly approve of the colors for actual wear. A green dress with pink and slate-color trimmings also looks well. If the kite is

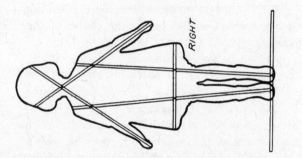

FIG. 18. OUTLINE FOR GIRL-WITH-SKIPPING-ROPE KITE

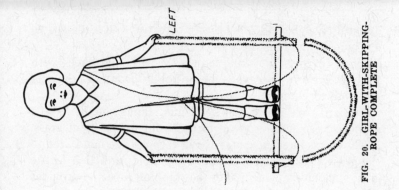

FIG. 19. FRAME FOR SKIPPING-GIRL KITE

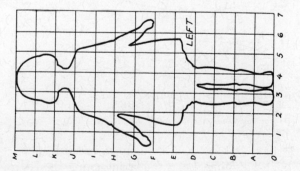

FIG. 20. GIRL-WITH-SKIPPING-ROPE COMPLETE

25

not stiff enough, fold some pieces of paper like those shown in Figure 4, and glue them in place.

Draw in the hair, skin, features, socks, and shoes with water colors or wax crayons. Draw boldly. Don't get the eyes too close together.

The stick on which the little girl stands should have a strip of green festoon glued to the front to represent grass. A white or colored festoon passing through the hand, tied to the grass stick, draped to the other hand, and tied to the grass stick on that side makes the skipping rope and provides the tail. A total of about 18 feet should be used.

Attach the bridle loop from the shoulder to the grass stick on the opposite side, just outside the skipping rope. The finished loops should be about 33 inches in length. The towing point falls over a point $3\frac{3}{4}$ inches below the center of the chin and 12 inches from the surface of the kite.

Not counting the tail below the grass line, the above kite rated 1.32 ounces per square foot. It was a fair flier and was very pretty and graceful.

No. 8. The Fisherman

Draw the pattern as suggested for kites Nos. 5 and 6. Wire may be used for the greater part of the rod, covering with a strip of paper so it will be large enough to look like a fishing

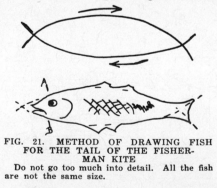

FIG. 21. METHOD OF DRAWING FISH
FOR THE TAIL OF THE FISHER-
MAN KITE
Do not go too much into detail. All the fish
are not the same size.

rod and still be light. A long stick is likely to break from a fall or from rough handling. Loop the string along the rod and make a bobber from a wad of crêpe paper tied into shape.

Cut a strip an inch wide round and round an old stocking for the tail. Pass it through the hand, and tie it fast to the bottom of the foot. The fishes should be made of wrapping

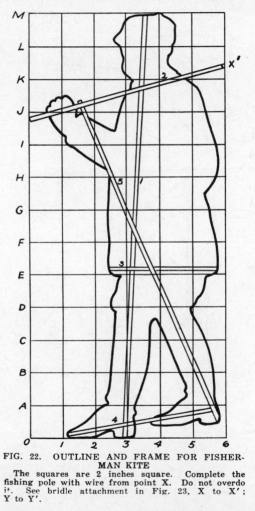

FIG. 22.   OUTLINE AND FRAME FOR FISHER-
MAN KITE
The squares are 2 inches square.   Complete the fishing pole with wire from point X.   Do not overdo it.   See bridle attachment in Fig. 23, X to X';
Y to Y'.

paper colored to suit. They are best made double, like a sack, and kept partly distended by scraps of tissue paper stuffed into them. Put them on the string at intervals of a foot running the string through the mouth and out of the gills. Secure

with a daub of glue. Prepare about 20 feet of tail with 15 or
20 fishes, finishing off with a turtle made in the same manner
as the fish. If more weight is required, a teaspoonful of earth

FIG. 23.   FISHERMAN
KITE COMPLETE

in some of the fishes, starting with the one at the bottom,
will provide all the weight that is needed. Color the features
and clothing to conform with the fishing sport.

Attach a bridle by running a loop from X to Y, and another loop from X' to Y'. Gather the loops with a tow string, and adjust the whole bridle so that the towing point falls over point A, about 12 inches from the surface of the kite. Use the trough-shape reënforcements shown in Figure 4 where needed. Do not try to fly the kite until quite dry.

The Fisherman Kite rated 1.51 ounces per square foot. The flying power was fair, but not as light and dainty as the Girl With Skipping Rope. It caused lots of fun for the neighborhood kite fliers.

No. 9. THE ELEPHANT

Follow the diagram. Construct the kite using gray paper for the elephant and gay colors for the howdah and trimmings. The eye, tusk, and ear should be accented with black and white. Observe the directions given for the preceding kites for treatment of sticks and framing. The sticks need

FIG. 24. OUTLINE FOR ELEPHANT KITE
The squares are 2 by 2 inches.

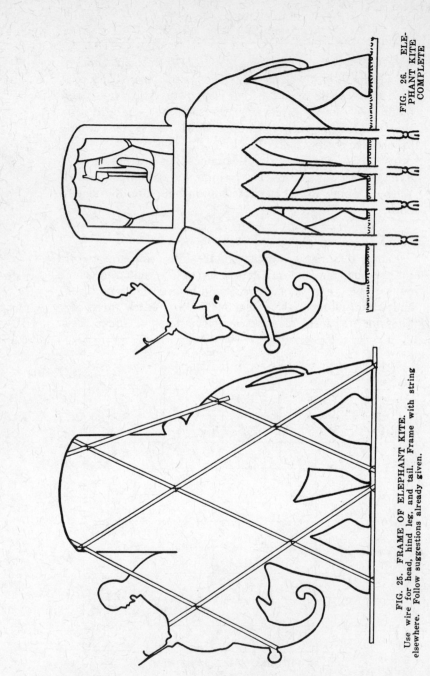

FIG. 25. FRAME OF ELEPHANT KITE.
Use wire for head, hind leg, and tail. Frame with string elsewhere. Follow suggestions already given.

FIG. 26. ELE-PHANT KITE COMPLETE

not be over 3/16 of an inch wide. Suggestions for stiffening the paper are given in the Introduction and in Figure 4. The ground stick should be covered with green festooning or tissue cut fine as described for kite No. 7. The howdah drapery forms the tail. Use four pieces of 1½-inch festoon, 8 feet long. Drape from the front of the kite, tying to the grass stick. Even the ends and attach tissue-paper tassels, if desired.

Run a bridle loop from the end of the stick forming the angle of the head to the end of the stick in the hindermost foot; and another loop from the foremost foot to the stick ending just above the tail. Or, the bridle may be attached as in No. 7, running the loops from points on the grass stick just outside the feet to the top of the howdah. In either case, the towing point should be about 15 inches from the surface of the kite and in a line joining the intersections of the howdah and middle-feet sticks about 3 inches below the elephant's back line.

An Elephant Kite, made according to these directions, rated .90 ounce per square foot. It was an excellent flier.

No. 10. A Balloon Kite

Prepare a frame as for the two-stick kite, using a 26-inch stick for the spine and a 17-inch stick for the cross. The sticks should be about ¼ inch wide. Slit the ends making the slit wide enough to accommodate a No. 18 wire. Prepare another cross stick 12 inches long and ¼ inch wide and glue and lash it at right angles to the foot of the spine. The upper cross should be fixed at about 8 inches from the top of the spine.

Leaving about a foot of wire free, take a turn around the lower cross stick about 4 inches from the spine, run to the slit in the upper cross and thence to the slit at the top of the spine. Lay the incomplete frame on a large sheet of paper and shape the wire to conform to the half outline of a balloon. When satisfactory, mark the position of the curve and sticks with a pencil, turn the frame over and fit the sticks to the mark and shape the wire on this side to fit the curve

drawn from the wire of the other side. Let the wire extend
about a foot beyond the lower cross stick and snip off.

Wrap the ends and paper the kite in the usual manner.

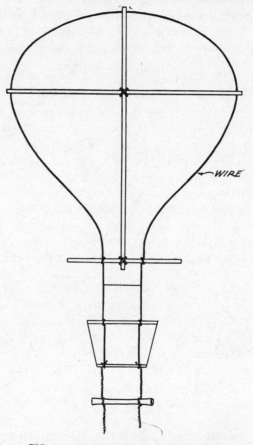

FIG. 27.   FRAME FOR BALLOON KITE
    Some kitemakers like a balloon of a little different shape. Plan your own
balloon, and attach the bridle from your knowledge of the other kites. The
whole outline is shaped with wire, and trough-shaped reenforcements as described in the introduction are used where needed.

Draw the ends of the wire together and fasten to a stick,
about 5 inches apart. A stick 8 inches long run between the
wires about 4 inches above this last stick makes the outline
for the basket. Paper the basket in fancy colors.

Cut about a dozen sticks 3/16 of an inch wide and 6 inches long. Small twigs may be used. Make a ladder using the short sticks for steps and two stocking strings for the sides. Place the steps about 6 inches apart, tying fast to the sides with twine. The ladder may end in several feet of knotted string. The step part should be about 6 feet long. Use more sticks if necessary. Attach the ladder for a tail by tying to the lower corners of the basket.

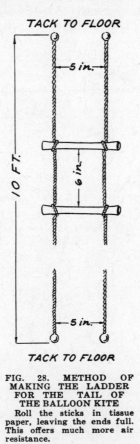

FIG. 28. METHOD OF MAKING THE LADDER FOR THE TAIL OF THE BALLOON KITE
Roll the sticks in tissue paper, leaving the ends full. This offers much more air resistance.

The bridle is made as described in the Two-Stick Kite, the towing point falling about 5 inches below the top of the kite and 15 inches from its surface.

The projecting ends of the lower cross stick may carry small flags or parachutes.

The Balloon made from the above specifications weighed, without flags, parachutes, or tail, .67 ounces per square foot. It proved a good flier.

For directions for making parachutes, see Chapter VI.

Ten plane-surface kites have been described in detail. If four or five of these have been made with some degree of success, you may now proceed to the next chapter on Tailless Kites and be equally successful.

Chapter III

TAILLESS KITES

A fact often overlooked in flying a kite is that many forces and restraints operate to make the flight successful. I do not know any common example to which the flight of a kite may be compared. Many writers compare the performance of a kite with that of a sailing vessel, but a short discussion will enable us to see that the kite and ship have little in common.

In the first place, even in the case of the tallest masts, the sails remain very near the surface of the water where the direction and force of the wind is fairly constant in a limited area at a given time. A ship moves, and moves at a velocity proportional to the wind. A ship's sidewise movements are greatly limited, although there may be considerable rolling.

A kite flies at an altitude where the direction of the wind, not only with respect to the compass, but also with respect to ascent and descent, varies moment by moment and must, therefore, be considered. For years, the soaring and gliding of birds was a great puzzle to naturalists until the existence of rising currents of air became known. It is now quite generally believed that soaring birds balance themselves on rapidly rising columns of air. The strange cold storms of the Mediterranean Sea are but descending columns of cold air of gigantic size.

The rising columns of air enable us to fly a well-made kite on hot days when there is but little breeze at the surface. Just a short time ago, I sent up a train of three bow kites (No. 11) near a small tract of woodland. The flying was fair, but not entirely satisfactory. I was unable to get the leader into a higher current of air that I knew existed from the behavior of an airplane not far distant. While I was attempting to crowd the kites higher, the middle kite drifted over the woodland and immediately fell, snapping the string between me and the kites. The trees evidently checked the upward currents that had sustained the kites. The leader remained flying since it was over the bed of a dried-up pond, and the heated air could be seen quivering up from the surface. The third kite was at the nearer edge of the woodland, just where the horizontal currents were bent upward adding their force to the vertical currents. This kite immediately climbed to an altitude as high as that reached by the leader, broke away from the others and drifted nearly a mile away where I found it being studied by a number of cows.

One can get an excellent idea of the nature of air currents aloft if a box of finely torn paper or confetti is sent up and opened as described in Chapter VI. I have read that the United States Forest Service uses kites to liberate tree seeds from a height in order to study the effect of air currents on the distribution of seed.

We may say, therefore, that the currents of air encountered by a kite are exceedingly complex and variable as compared to those encountered by a sailing vessel.

A kite's forward motion is checked by the string and is not proportional to the wind, although its upward motion may be so to some extent. But this upward motion is not due to the release of the string, but to the reaction coming after the release has been slowed up or checked. In case of a ship, the movement is greatest in the direction of least resistance or where the restraint is the least. The kite's horizontal movements, unlike those of a ship, may be very great and still interfere but little with good flying, while rolling is practically unknown except in kites designed to perform antics or those out of balance. Both ship and kite pitch and dart, but from different causes. Still, it is not far wrong to compare the flight of a kite with the progress of a sailing vessel, provided that the vessel is dragging her anchor and is moving upward across a current flowing diagonally to the wind.

Kitemaking is unlike shipbuilding since the medium in which the kite sails is the same as that which propels it. Flying a motored plane or a glider is not to be compared with kite flying, since there is power in the motored plane and the lack of string in the glider.

I have planned kites for special purposes, and have resorted to higher mathematics and the principles of engineering to allow for every known and probable force. But I have, invariably, been surprised at their behavior on being sent up the first time. The kites usually flew, but like fancy fireworks (which usually go off), they hardly ever did just what was expected or planned.

To overcome all this uncertainty, I have tried out the kites I am describing, and I hope that, after the boys or girls gain confidence, they will accept the challenge of the air, make other kites and tinker with them until satisfactory fliers are obtained.

The kites described in this chapter offer an endless opportunity for alteration, so that practically any figure may be represented with a little skill and an abundance of patience.

No. 11. A Bow or Malay

Bow kites are those having the cross sticks sprung into a bow while the spines are nearly straight. The convex (outside) curvature is next to the flier, although, now and then, one sees a curious kite with the curve turned the other way. They are probably poor fliers and the curiosity lies in the fact that one cannot tell what they are going to do next.

The purpose of the convex bow is to take advantage of the spine for a keel, and to keep the kite surface properly shaped to catch the wind.

The people of the Malay Peninsula have used this kind of kite for many centuries, but it is thought that they borrowed the idea from the natives of Java who were, for a long time, the most expert kitemakers in the world.

Eddy, Woglom, Kirby, and others in the United States either independently discovered or perfected the Malay kite until its performance is little short of marvelous. Each professional kitemaker has some little detail that distinguishes his kite from the others, and which was probably worked out with much thought and experimentation. It is said that Eddy made his cross stick longer than the spine, that Woglom held invariably to the depth of the bow being

10 per cent of the length of the spine, and that Kirby made spine and cross equal with a greater bow, and called his kites "bird kites" from their proportions being like those of a bird. The kite described below is somewhat generalized from the various makers and is a most satisfactory flier.

Prepare two sticks 3/16 my ¼ by 26 inches and slit the ends as described in the Two-Stick Kite. Select a stick that bends uniformly for the bow. Both sticks must be straight and free from weakening imperfections.

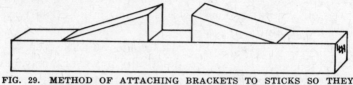

FIG. 29.　METHOD OF ATTACHING BRACKETS TO STICKS SO THEY MAY BE FASTENED TOGETHER WITH STRING ALONE
Both the spine and cross stick are to have brackets.

From each end of the cross stick, measure 12⅞ inches, and mark all around. From the top end of the spine, measure and mark at 5 and 5¼ inches. You will note that the length of the kite, inside of the slits, is 25 inches, and that the distance from the end of the slit to the top of the cross stick is 4½ inches or 18 per cent of the effective length.

From a stick the same width and thickness as those of the kite, cut four pieces an inch long. Lay one of these, flat side down, on a board, square one end and bevel the other making a little bracket about ¾ inch in length. Using this piece as a model, shape the other three sticks like it.

Lay the spine and cross stick in position, making sure the marks are right, but do not glue or wrap. Spread a little glue on the long face of a bracket and place it on the top mark of the spine as shown in Figure 29. Wrap well. Now lay the cross stick in place and fasten the bracket below the cross stick in the same manner. The brackets are to prevent the movement of the cross stick up and down, but they are to be free enough to allow its ready removal. The proper degree of looseness may be secured by wrapping a piece of paper around the cross stick and fitting closely. When the brackets are in place, the cross stick is withdrawn and the paper discarded. The paper allows enough play, and prevents the glue from getting on the cross stick.

Wipe off all excess glue, and bracket the cross stick in the same manner. Now tie the sticks together crisscross, finishing off with a knot that may be easily untied. You now have an intersection that is firm, but easily taken apart for carrying or storing. Start wrapping the ends of the sticks. The cross stick is not wrapped outside the framing string, so it may be finished off with an extra turn.

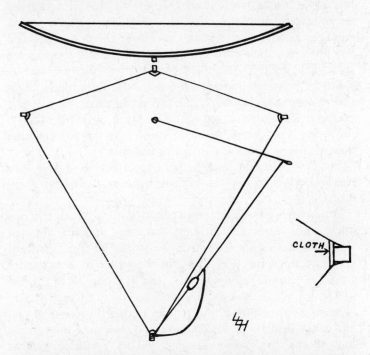

CLOTH→

FIG. 30. OUTLINE OF THE BOW KITE, FRONT AND TOP VIEW
The top view shows the proper amount of bow. The small sketch to the right shows the cloth reënforcement at the stick ends.

Frame the kite, making the necessary adjustments to make the sides equal. Do not draw the framing string tighter than is necessary to keep it straight. Take a stitch through the framing string ¾ of an inch inside the slits so the kite will present an outline as shown in Figure 30.

Paper the kite, spine next to the paper, and let it dry. Clip the stitches taken in the framing string and pull out the threads. Finish wrapping the ends of the spine.

Lay the kite paper side down. Attach a strong bow string securely to one end of the cross just inside the framing string, tying so it will lead off from the center of the stick. It should be considerably longer than the kite is wide. Make a square loop of wire that will slip over the other end of the cross stick, but will not slide down the stick when a pull is exerted on it at an angle. Twist the ends of the wire together six or eight turns and clip off. Now run the bow string through the wire loop, slip the wire over the cross stick and bow the cross stick until the distance from the string to the stick at the center is about 3 inches.

Catch the string and wire together with thumb and finger and remove from the stick. Tie the string to the wire in this position. Replace, and see if the distance from the stick to the string is between 2½ and 3 inches. If not, readjust so the bow will be as near these limits as possible.

Let down the bow, and prepare to attach the bridle. Use elastic bridles on tailless kites, whenever their shape will permit.

Run a string through the paper at the intersection of the sticks and tie securely around the spine and bracket just below the cross stick. The string must lead off from the front center of the spine. Tie a loop in the string so the distance from the kite to the knot will be just 13 inches. Run the end of the string under the wrapping at the lower end of the spine as described for kite No. 1, and bring the length of this end of the bridle to 21 inches measured from the knot in the loop to the kite. Preserving the lengths, tie in the rubber band about 4 inches from the bottom. Be sure to attach the safety string. You will need it more on this kite than on those heretofore described. No horizontal bridle is required.

The paper just inside the stick ends should be reënforced with a strip of cloth as wide as the finger. Paste the cloth, lay it in position on the face of the kite, and turn it over the edges. If the color is objectionable, cover it with kite paper.

The place where the bridle passes through the paper should be reënforced with a circular patch clipped to allow the string to lead through it. This may be put on the back of the kite.

When dry, you will have a kite that will fly in any breeze, and with a bit more bow in a strong wind. No tail is needed, although streamers and flags may be attached as described in Chapter VI.

I have made a large number of kites from the above specifications, and every one was a strong flier. Crêpe paper makes the flight more steady. For a kite this size, crêpe paper weighs but 1/7 of an ounce more than plain tissue, and gives a much better performance. The crêpe-paper kite rated .42 ounce and the plain-paper kite rated .44 ounce per square foot.

No. 12. TETRAHEDRAL KITE

A tetrahedron, from which the word tetrahedral is derived, means a solid bounded by four surfaces. In the kite, only two of the surfaces are utilized. A little experimenting will demonstrate that the sides must be triangular. The old puzzle to make four triangles with six matches will serve as an explanation. Lay three matches in the form of a triangle on a table. Hold three other matches between the thumb and fingers, and place the free ends at each angle of the triangle and you have solved the puzzle. If a kite frame is made on the same principle and any two sides are papered, a tetrahedral cell or kite unit is formed.

Doctor Alexander Graham Bell made serious attempts with huge kites made of tetrahedral units to solve the problem of airplane construction and much discussion of the principles was to be found in the magazines between the years 1903 and 1908. I have not found the single units to be as satisfactory as the bow kite, and the United States Weather Bureau has not found them to be as satisfactory for their work as the box kite perfected by Professor Martin. Since the tetrahedral principle is much used in making figure kites, the method for making a tetrahedral cell or unit is described in the following pages.

Since the arrangement of the sticks forms an ideal system of bracing, the sticks may be much smaller in width and thickness than those required for other kinds of kites having the same amount of surface. Prepare seven sticks ¼ by ¼ by 26 inches. Lay them on a table so two equilateral triangles are formed and one stick left over. Many ingenious plans have been devised to use six sticks and still provide for folding, but to use the extra stick is the easiest and, in general,

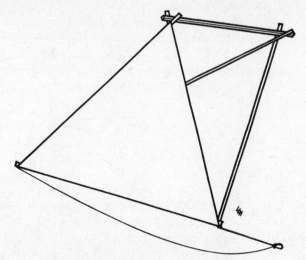

FIG. 31. TETRAHEDRAL KITE COMPLETE

the most satisfactory. Pare away the wood at the ends, so the triangles will lie flat on the table without rocking. Do not let the ends lap over ½ inch. Glue and tie. Lay one triangle over the other and match up the size, shape, and weight. Remove and allow to dry. Decide which sides of the triangle are to join, and glue a strip of paper to form a hinge while the triangular frames are spread open, and press to position after the frames have been carefully closed. Allow the hinge to dry. Now paper the sides, framework in, and spread the two papered triangles apart and hold in position by lashing the extra stick fast to their upper angles.

Care should be exercised to get the paper at the same tension so the triangles will not be drawn out of shape.

There are various ways of attaching the bridle. One of the simplest ways is to attach a single string to one end of the hinge, and attach the kite line to this string. However, the

A TETRAHEDRAL KITE
The above tetrahedral kite is one of which the boy is justly proud. It is a cell kite of which only two surfaces are utilized, resulting in a triangular shape.

following is a better method: Cut a string twice as long as the hinge, and tie a loop about one fourth the length of the string. Tie the kite line into the loop, and tie the longer end of the string to the far end of the hinge, and the shorter end to the near end of the hinge. The loop may be too far back, causing the kite to pull flat against the wind. In this case, the kite will not rise. The object in making the string long is to provide for adjustments.

Some patience and a stiff breeze will be necessary for a successful flight. These kites perform remarkably well in a strong wind, and will stand a very great amount of abuse. After a flight, untie the top stick and fold the kite together.

A kite, made according to the above directions, rated 1 ounce per square foot. Since the wings were set at an angle of 60 degrees, the effective surface was only about half the actual surface. It is, therefore, easy to see why this type of kite is adapted to strong winds: it has relatively a small effective surface with great strength and stability. Figure 31 shows the completed kite. If a larger tetrahedral kite is desired, follow the picture on page 43, making the cells the size of the one just described.

No. 13.   An Owl

Prepare two sticks ⅛ by ¼ by 26 inches from whitewood. Prepare another stick a bit thinner about 15 inches long. These sticks are bent after the manner described under the English kite (p. 15). For the frame proper, prepare two sticks ¼ inch square, one 26 inches, and the other 15 inches long. Another ¼-inch stick about 6 inches long and a slightly thinner one of the same length will also be needed.

Bend the sticks as shown, both at the same time, if possible, and allow them to dry before releasing them from the form. The thinner stick should be bent into a semicircle, and wet again with hot water when you are ready to shape the kite. Draw the outline of the owl on paper to size, and fold over so both sides will be alike. It may be well to trace the curve for the forms from the pattern. Lash and glue the sticks in position as shown in Figure 32, but do not fasten the cross stick to the edges of the kite until after the kite is papered. Paper with buff paper, cutting out large eyes and making spectral eyes for the bird as described for the Imp Kite (p. 23). Yellow school paper when greased makes splendid eyes for this kite. Finish the eyes with black centers.

When dry, tie the cross stick to the edges of the kite so the paper is about 3 inches from the intersection of the spine and cross stick. Thrust the remaining stick through the paper just in front of, and a little below the cross stick, allowing it to project downward. Tie a string to the front end of this stick, and draw the string to the top of the spine and tie off. Paper the triangle thus formed making a beak. This beak is very necessary, since the kite is not a true bow kite, and it needs a keel to keep it straight.

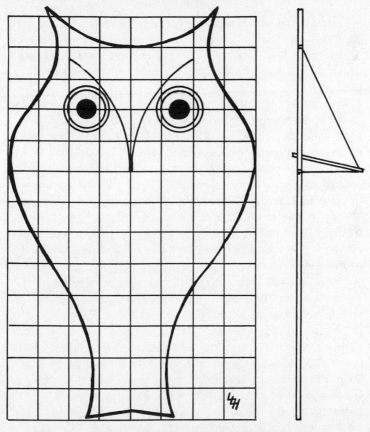

FIG. 32. FRONT AND EDGE VIEWS OF THE OWL KITE
The squares are 2 by 2 inches.

The Owl Kite may be flown with a single bridle attached to the tip of the beak, but it flies better with a bridle attached like the Bow Kite. There is no objection to using a side bridle, if there is a tendency toward excessive rocking.

Draw in the features of the bird boldly with black, white, and yellow. Remember that the under parts of a bird are lighter in color than the butts of the wings or back.

The Owl Kite rated .94 ounce per square foot. It was a good flier.

No. 14. A Frog

We have all observed the prominent hump in the small part of a frog's back. Turning this hump to practical use in designing a kite, we are able to make a prominent keel which with a little bowing keeps the kite steady without a tail.

Two sticks, ¼ by ¼ by 26 inches, and another ¼ by ¼ by 20 inches are required. A fourth stick may be made a little wider and 6 inches long. Arrange the three long sticks as shown in Figure 33; frame and paper the kite with white or light gray paper, using the V-shape reënforcements described in Figure 4 where needed. If you care to use a piece of wire for the head, wrap the wire around one diagonal, thence to the tip of the spine and to the other diagonal, wrapping and finishing off as in the Imp (p. 23). The other curves will hardly need wire. Let the toes be free to vibrate in the wind.

Thrust the remaining stick through the paper just over the intersection of the sticks, and glue and lash it fast to the sticks. Attach a string to the tip of the spine (nose) and run it through a slit in the short stick just put in place and from thence to the tail. Paper the triangle thus formed, holding it perpendicular to the surface of the kite if need be by small strips of paper or by running a string to the edge of the figure. Color the frog appropriately with green and black spots, paint in the eyes and claws, and attach a bridle from the nose to the tail and from one fore leg to the other. There should be a bow string across the back of the kite connecting the fore feet and another connecting the hind feet. The bow should be fully 3 inches.

If a light thread is attached to each hind foot and allowed to trail to the ground, many interesting stunts may be performed giving the appearance of leaps and swimming strokes when the threads are managed by an assistant. This kite is very striking, and has great possibilities of development. A kite, made according to the above directions weighed .98 ounce per square foot. It was a good flier.

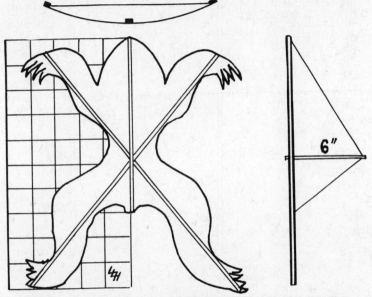

FIG. 33. FRONT AND EDGE VIEW OF THE FROG KITE BEFORE BOWING

The small sketch above the Frog shows the proper amount of bow. Both the front and hind legs will require bow strings.

No. 15. A Shield

Use is again made of the bow in the Shield Kite, although bowing alone is not sufficient to make the kite steady. Unlike the Bow Kite, the Shield Kite is top-heavy and needs a keel to keep it upright.

A keel in front would spoil the effect of the shield so the keel may be put on the back of the kite. Follow the suggestions given for the Frog Kite for making the keel (See p. 46).

Using bunting crêpe paper, the kite may be made according to the pattern shown in Figure 34. The keel should be supported by a light stick lashed to the intersection of the upright and bow stick. It need not extend backward over 8 inches.

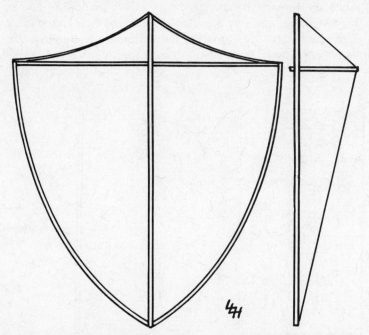

FIG. 34. FRONT AND EDGE VIEWS OF THE SHIELD KITE FRAME
Observe that the keel is on the back of this kite.

The stripes and stars will have to be cut and joined in the proper position according to the outline of the shield. The usual width of the stripes to be had in paper found on sale is 1.7 inches which makes the greatest possible width at the bottom of the blue field about 22 inches. The sticks required are:

1 Spine   ¼ by ¼ by 26 inches,
1 Cross   ¼ by ¼ by 23 inches,
2 Sides 3/32 by ¼ by 26 inches,
1 Keel   ¼ by ¼ by 8 inches.

Paper the kite, bow it, and attach the keel. Paper the keel with red, white, and blue if it extends the length of the kite, or with red and white stripes if it extends only from the intersection of the principal sticks to the bottom of the spine.

Attach a bridle, following the suggestions given for the Malay Kite, keeping the towing point as high as possible. No exact figures can be given, as a slight flare in the side sticks alters the behavior of a Shield Kite considerably. It may be necessary to bend the side sticks with hot water as described for the English Kite. Usually, if the side sticks are thin and sound, they may be held in shape with a string.

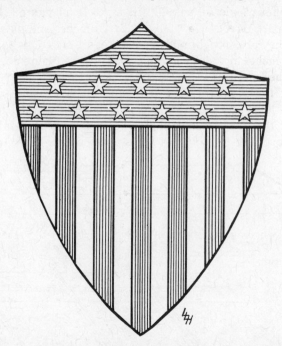

FIG. 35. FRONT VIEW OF THE COMPLETED SHIELD KITE
The bridle is attached in the same manner as that of the Bow Kite.

Kites of this type are very pretty, but do not fly so well as those made with rattan and bamboo sticks. A kite, made according to Figures 34 and 35, weighed 1.08 ounce per square foot. It was a good flier; in fact, in a class with the Star Kites and the Imp.

No. 16. A Triangular Box Kite

Box kites give the boys and girls a chance to show their skill. They are not hard to make, but those that are carefully made fly ever so much better than those that are carelessly put together.

The Triangular Box Kite does not have as good a rating as the other box kites. There is more weight per unit of lifting surface, since a clumsier arrangement is required to keep the sides taut. But triangular box kites fly very well, and they offer wonderful possibilities as keels for figure kites.

Prepare three sticks ¼ by ¼ by 26 inches and make sure that they are straight and sound. Prepare six sticks ¼ by ¼ by 15 inches and sharpen them as shown in Figure 36. Make sure the lengths are exactly the same.

Cut two strips of thin firm paper 8 inches wide and 47 inches long. Lay the two papers on the floor parallel to each other, the outside edges being 25 inches apart. Make the ends even, so a stick laid across the ends will be at right

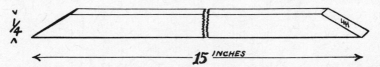

FIG. 36. SKETCH OF THE DISTENTION STICK FOR THE TRIANGULAR BOX KITE

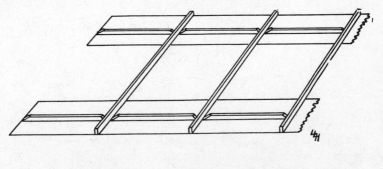

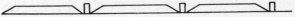

FIG. 37. PERSPECTIVE AND END VIEW OF THE METHOD OF ATTACHING THE STICKS TO THE PAPER OF THE TRIANGULAR BOX KITE

angles (square) with the edges. Glue the sticks to the paper as shown in Figure 37. Be sure to keep the long sticks at right angles to the strips of paper and not to let the papers slip on the floor. Let the kite dry a few hours, join the ends of the paper as shown in Figure 38, and attach a bridle at point "A." Kites made as above are not collapsible.

The Triangular Box Kite made from the above directions presented an effective surface to the wind of about one half the edges of the "V" and about one half the back wall; all told, about 360 square inches. It weighed 1.20 ounces per square foot. It was an excellent kite for flying in a strong wind.

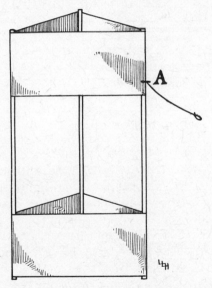

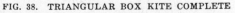

FIG. 38. TRIANGULAR BOX KITE COMPLETE

No. 17. A Square Box Kite

The history of the Square Box Kite is full of interest to all kitemakers. The box kite was invented, about 1892, by Hargrave, an Australian, who later hoped to develop the kite for lifting observers. The idea was not new, as the Chinese and Japanese both have stories of man-lifting kites of great antiquity. While man-lifting kites have been made and tried for military purposes, the principal value of the box kite lies in its use for studying the conditions of the upper atmosphere. It is interesting to note that the Western people in the space of twenty years, invented and perfected a much better kite when they developed the box kite, than the Eastern peoples, long regarded as expert kitemakers, have done in twenty centuries. The rectangular box kite is the usual type used for scientific purposes, but the square box still remains a great favorite for amusement.

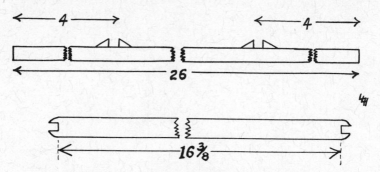

FIG. 39. SKETCHES OF UPRIGHT AND DIAGONAL STICKS OF THE SQUARE BOX KITE

The proportions, 12 by 12 by 26 inches with paper 7 inches wide, are ideal. Reënforcement is hardly necessary if good-quality, light-weight wrapping paper is used. A string dipped in thin glue and applied to the paper will give enough reenforcement should any be found necessary.

Prepare four sticks ⅛ by ⅜ by 26 inches and four others ⅛ by ⅜ by 17½ inches. Glue chips on the long sticks and notch the short sticks as shown in Figure 39.

Prepare two strips of paper, 7 by 49 inches each, and lay them over each other smoothly and evenly. Fold the two ends together, letting one end project 1 inch beyond the other. Crease down carefully. Now bring the creased center over to the shorter end and crease down. Turn the 1-inch end back and crease down. Unfold the papers. The creases should be equidistant from each other, 12 inches apart, and at right angles to the margins.

Lay the papers on the floor parallel to each other, the outer edges 25 inches apart. The creases indicate the positions of the sticks.

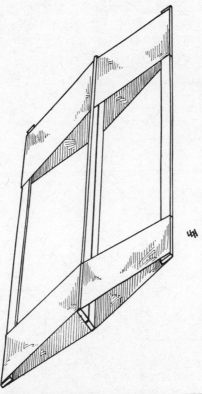

FIG. 40. PERSPECTIVE VIEW OF THE SQUARE BOX KITE LET DOWN SHOWING HOW STICKS SHOULD BE SPACED

Apply glue to the edges of the sticks opposite the chips, and press the first stick along the crease of the paper at the end having the 1-inch projection. The stick is to be between the crease and the end. Attach the other sticks at the following creases, keeping the sticks on the same sides of the creases as the first. In other words, starting at the 1-inch projection, the order will be: end of paper, stick, crease, stick, crease, stick, crease, stick, other end of paper. Let the kite dry. Then bring the two ends of the paper together, sticks on the inside, so the sticks will have the same distance apart throughout. The kite should now appear like Figure 40.

If you have measured correctly, your cross sticks will fit as shown in Figure 41, but do not attempt to fit them until the kite is dry and firm. The cross sticks will fit snugly enough to hold the kite out correctly. The cross sticks should be tied together.

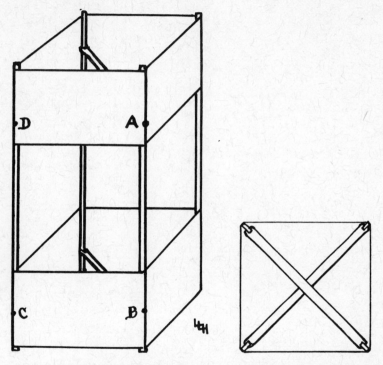

FIG. 41. PERSPECTIVE AND END VIEWS OF THE SQUARE BOX KITE

Attach a single-string bridle at A (Fig. 41), and the kite is ready to fly. When through flying, remove the cross sticks and fold up.

These kites have wonderful flying behavior, being surpassed only by the bow kite. They require so little attention that the string may be tied to a fence and the kite will remain aloft.

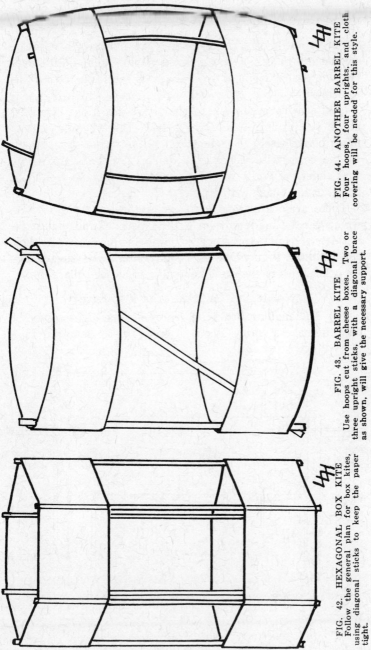

FIG. 42. HEXAGONAL BOX KITE. Follow the general plan for box kites, using diagonal sticks to keep the paper tight.

FIG. 43. BARREL KITE. Use hoops cut from cheese boxes. Two or three upright sticks, with a diagonal brace as shown, will give the necessary support.

FIG. 44. ANOTHER BARREL KITE. Four hoops, four uprights, and cloth covering will be needed for this style.

55

For strong winds, the kite may be flown with a bridle attached to points A, B, C, D, the towing point falling over the line drawn from A to B about as far from the kite as its length.

A kite made according to the above directions rated .93 ounce per square foot (two sides) if flown sidewise. If flown cornerwise, the rating was .60 ounce per square foot. In the cornerwise rating, the diagonal was multiplied by four times the width of the paper since both the front and back surfaces have lifting power.

There are many modifications of the Square Box Kite which can be made with a little experimenting. They are not described in detail since no new principle is used in their construction. Figures 42 to 44 may offer some suggestions for other kites of the same general plan as the square box.

No. 18.   A Rectangular Box Kite

The Rectangular Box Kite represents the highest type of the kitemakers' skill. There is considerable material in a

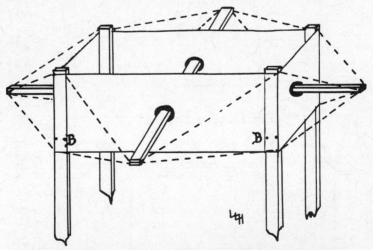

FIG. 45.   VIEW OF ONE END OF A RECTANGULAR BOX KITE
The dotted lines show strings running from the corners to the tightening sticks.

kite of this kind, so naturally there is a size that has the highest rating and the best flying performance. The weather

bureaus of the United States and foreign countries agree
that a height of 6 to 8 feet and a depth of about 1/3 of the
height is the ideal size for high and severe flights. The widths

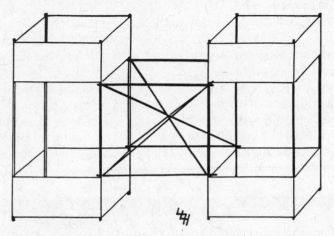

FIG. 46. TWO SQUARE BOX KITES CONNECTED IN TANDEM
If long sticks are at hand, they may run clear through the kites. The
lattice bracing need not then be used.

vary somewhat as do the widths of the paper or cloth. The
average dimensions of seven United States and foreign kites
reduced to the size possible to make from orange-crate sticks
are as follows:

Height, 26 inches; width, 22 inches; depth, 8¾ inches;
width of paper, 7¼ inches.

The top cell should be divided crosswise. It is possible that
some trouble will be had in keeping the sides taut with
diagonal sticks alone, and since there is to be a divided cell
at the top, it may be well to use six uprights and brace the
kite as if it were two square box kites side by side. In fact,
some kitemakers make their rectangular box kites from two
or more square kites, cutting away the surplus paper after
the kites are joined together. Another plan sometimes used
is to stay the corners to sticks by means of strings as shown
in Figure 45. Two sticks may be used instead of four if
longer material is available, allowing a liberal length to
project beyond each end of the kite. If the kite is to be kept

set up, nothing more than carefully fitted diagonals are needed. If two square box kites are to be joined, it is better to carry them on a framework some distance apart as shown in Figure 46.

Detailed directions are not given for making this kite, since its construction does not differ from the other box kites and any thoughtful boy or girl can set it up from the dimensions and description.

The kite is to be flown flat side to the wind. A bridle loop twice the length of the kite attached at points BB is usually sufficient, although some kitemakers prefer long loops running from the opposite corners of the front surface. In this case, the towing point should fall in the center line about one fourth or one fifth the distance from the top.

U. S. WEATHER BUREAU KITE

Kites are used not only for fun and sport, but are also instrumental in forecasting weather conditions. The above kite, used by the United States Weather Bureau is equipped with a meteorograph which simultaneously records the barometric pressure, temperature, moisture, wind, rainfall, sunshine, evaporation, etc.   (U. S. Weather Bureau)

A kite made from the dimensions on page 57, using plain diagonals glued to the sticks and glued at the intersections, rated .90 ounce per square foot. It was not as graceful in flight as the bow kite, nor as responsive as the square box, still it was an excellent flier and had wonderful lifting power. Weather Bureau kites are of this style.

TWO VIEWS OF U. S. WEATHER BUREAU KITE
Two views of landing a kite used by the U. S. Weather Bureau in making forecasts.
(U. S. Weather Bureau)

No. 19.   A Butterfly Kite

The Butterfly Kite is, in reality, a double Tetrahedral Kite
appropriately colored and trimmed. Make the frame as

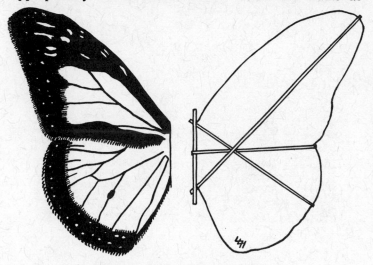

FIG. 47.   THE BUTTERFLY KITE

Outline of markings and framing plan.   Remember the lower sides of the
wings are the sides that are seen.

shown in Figure 47. Study the common butterflies in your
vicinity for suggestions on shape and decoration and fit the
frame to conform to the shape selected. While the wings are
attached to a hinge arrangement as in the Tetrahedral Kite,
there is no need of having the attachment stiff and rigid.
Make the hinge of cloth, allowing plenty of play so the
flight will be light and airy. The wings should be held apart
by an elastic-stick arrangement as shown in Figure 49. This
will allow the wings to flutter, and will give a fair represen-
tation of flying. A body with legs and feelers may be made
if desired. Tie strings around the crêpe-paper body to divide
it into the three insect parts; head, thorax, and abdomen.
The legs and wings are borne on the thorax and the feelers
or antennæ on the head. Study a butterfly for suggestions.
Stiffening may be worked out according to Figure 4, and the
suggestions given in the Introduction.

I have made butterfly kites with a twist in the sticks that form the upper tip of the forewing and the lower tip of the opposite hind wing that performed all sorts of zigzag motions. I usually make the tails of the butterfly's wing slender enough so they do not interfere with a steady flight.

FIG. 48. THE BUTTERFLY KITE WHILE FLYING
The tips of the wings should be about as far apart as the distance from the wing tip to the body.

I made a butterly kite after the Monarch Butterfly, and found it to be a good flier. Since the wings moved somewhat, offering a varying amount of surface to the wind, I did not attempt to rate it as I did the other kites. However, the longest sticks were ¼ by ¼ by 26 inches, and the completed kite weighed 3 ounces.

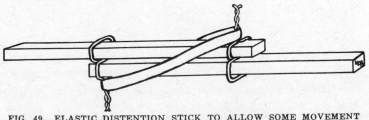

FIG. 49. ELASTIC DISTENTION STICK TO ALLOW SOME MOVEMENT TO THE WINGS OF THE BUTTERFLY KITE
The total length should be about the same as the distance from tip of the wing to the body.

No. 20. A Yacht Kite

The Yacht Kite may be readily constructed by following Figures 50 and 51. The spine or "mast" should be ⅜ inch wide to a point just above the intersection of the diagonal sticks. From there, it may be tapered to ¼ inch square at the top. The total length of the spine is 26 inches. The diagonals are ¼ by ¼ by 20 inches. The "beam" of the hull is 9 inches and the upper yardarm 4 inches.

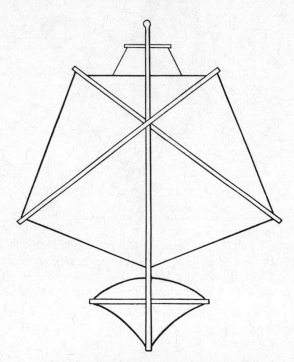

FIG. 50. FRAME OF THE YACHT KITE

The hull outline may be made of wire, although rather thick shavings stiffened with a little glue, are preferable. Frame with string as shown, paper the hull with dark paper and the sail with white. Bow the kite about 2 inches at the top, and about 3½ inches at the bottom of the sails. The top sail need not be bowed.

Attach the bridle from the intersection of the sticks to the keel, keeping about the same proportions as in the case of the Bow Kite.

If the flying performance is not satisfactory, run a bowsprit forward from the intersection of the beam and mast about 10 inches and attach a "gib sail" as described for the

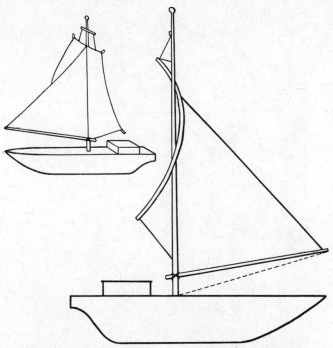

FIG. 51. TWO VIEWS OF THE YACHT KITE COMPLETE

keel of the Frog and Shield Kites. Do not forget to point the bowsprit upward so the tip will be on a line with the lower arms of the mainsail. The gib sail should not extend higher or lower than the mainsail. It is a good idea to let the top of the gib fall just below the bridle attachment and the bottom just above the bottom of the mainsails. If a gib is used, the bridle will have to be made much longer.

A kite made according to the above directions, rated 1.10 ounces per square foot. It proved an excellent flier.

Ten tailless kites have been described in this chapter, some of them easy to make and some of rather difficult construction. If you have made a few tailed kites and a few tailless

THE KITE USED IN LIEUT. COMMANDER BYRD'S POLAR EXPEDITION
Samuel F. Perkins, the government kitemaker, is shown attaching an aërial to one of the kites used by Lieut. Commander Byrd on his Polar expedition, to be used in case of a forced landing.   (Keystone View Co.)

kites, you are now ready to make the type of kites that include both plane surfaces and surfaces not in the same plane. Bird kites do not differ greatly from the butterfly kite, and fish kites are but modifications of the bow-kite principle.

The Chinese often make snake and dragon kites, made up of a large number of connected kites of bow type.

As a rule, we do not have patience enough to correct a kite with a faulty figure. I have known many excellent figure kites to be thrown away when just a few minutes of intelligent work would have made them successful fliers. The importance of keeping a record of your kites and the means employed to correct faulty flight cannot be overestimated. If I correct a faulty flier and forget how I did it, I must study out the means of correction every time I make a faulty flier. And if I do not remember how faults are corrected, or do not keep a record book, I shall forever be making faulty fliers.

I have given many cautions on flying kites before they have had time to dry. To attempt a flight when the paper is soft and the glue weak and the whole kite heavier than need be, is foolish. Reasonable patience and care will provide a means of acquiring much skill in one of the most ancient of outdoor sports.

Chapter IV

COMPOUND KITES

A number of kites have recently appeared in toy stores that have the elements of plane-surface kites combined with the elements of kites with more than one plane surface. Some fly very well, but many are indifferent fliers because the extra surface has been overdone. It has been mentioned elsewhere that the plane surface should not be greater than the surfaces not in the same plane, unless one wishes to attach a tail to the kite. It will be found a good plan to have the plane surfaces

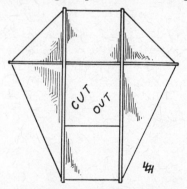

FIG. 52. BACK FRAME FOR THE TRI-
ANGULAR BOX KITE WITH WINGS
Observe that the square in the center is not papered.

or wings a little smaller than the surfaces of the box or keel part of the kite. If a Compound Kite is then unsatisfactory in flying behavior, it is probably because the open space in the center is too small. The open space in the keel or box part of a Compound Kite should be from one third to two thirds the length of the upright sticks. The bridle should be attached so the towing point is from one sixth to one fourth the length of the upright sticks from the top of the kite.

No. 21. TRIANGULAR BOX KITE WITH WINGS

This kite may be made like the Triangular Box Kite and the wings added, but I find the following way to be better:

Prepare four sticks 3/16 by 3/16 by 26 inches for uprights. Prepare one stick ¼ by ⅜ by 26 inches for the cross or wing spreader. Six sticks 3/16 by 3/16 by 10 inches complete the material for the frame.

Lay two uprights parallel to each other, 9 inches apart; even the ends and mark the sticks 9 inches from each end. Glue and lash the sticks in the position shown in Figure 52. Treat the framing and stick ends according to the method described for kite No. 1. Glue the paper to the sticks, and cut out the center of the kite as shown. It will be seen that the center panel of the kite is divided into thirds, the middle

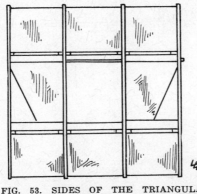

FIG. 53. SIDES OF THE TRIANGULAR KEEL ATTACHED TO THE BACK FRAME
Notice the sticks that hold the triangular box taut.

third being cut out. As a matter of fact, you will probably find that the kites fly a little better if the lower part of the center panel is a trifle more than a third. For a kite using 26-inch sticks, the upper part should be 8½ inches and the lower part about 9¼ inches wide.

Lay the kite on the floor, frame up, and attach the paper and the remaining sticks as shown in Figure 53. When dry, swing the sides of the box forward, tie the two forward sticks together in three or four places and the kite is ready for the bridle. Tie a tow string at the place designated by the circle and letter A in Figure 54. The towing point will have to be changed according to the strength of the wind, but it will always be from 4½ to 6½ inches from the top of the kite. The kite made from the foregoing description weighed .80 ounce per square foot. It was an excellent flier.

If wider wings are desired, a longer stick may be made by gluing and wrapping two sticks together for two or three

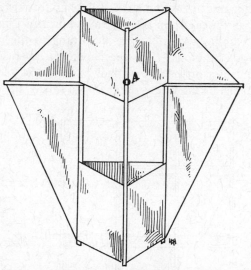

FIG. 54. TRIANGULAR BOX KITE WITH WINGS
COMPLETE
Towing point will fall near the place marked A.

inches, or a stick may be cut from other material. But remember the principle that the wings must be of less area than the box, unless you wish to fly the kite with a tail. The usefulness of this kind of kite to explorers is mentioned just below the illustration on page 64.

No. 22. A Square Box Kite with Wings

There is no easier way to make this strong-flying kite than first to make a box kite as described in No. 17, and to add the wings as shown in Figure 53. This method is not recommended for the Triangular Box Kite with Wings since it is desirable to make compound kites so they may be folded. Storage of kites is quite a problem at any time, and especially if the kite has considerable thickness. Since the kite about to be described may be folded, the stick supporting the wings being tied to the frame, it needs but little more space than the Square Box Kite itself.

The lifting power of kites of this kind is enormous, but sometimes they refuse to rise at all, especially in a strong wind. A long bridle must then be added as described for box kites. A little adjusting will then correct the trouble and the kite will tug at its string almost beyond belief. The kite is shown in Figure 55.

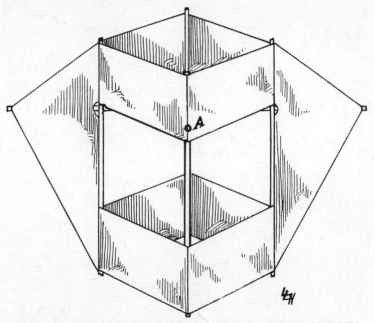

FIG. 55. CORNER VIEW OF THE SQUARE BOX KITE WITH WINGS
This kite may be flown in ordinary winds from the point marked by the letter A. For strong-wind flying, see the description of the kite for instructions.

A kite of the above type rated .50 ounce per square foot. It was an excellent flier.

No. 23. A MILITARY KITE

To construct the Military Kite shown in Figure 56, follow the directions for constructing the Rectangular Box Kite as described in No. 18, with the exception of those for making the sticks.

Cut four pairs of sticks ¼ by ⅜ by 24 inches, lap the ends of each pair about 4 inches, glue and wrap, making four sticks 44 inches long. Slit the ends.

Mark the sticks 11 inches from one end and tie the top of the *back* uprights of the kite at the place marked. Use the long sticks for diagonals, adjusting first one end and then the other of the kite until the kite is true and the corners square.

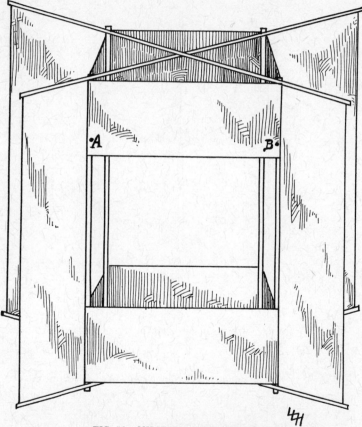

FIG. 56. MILITARY KITE SET UP

Attach bridle at points A and B. A bridle loop to the lower part of the kite may be necessary if the wind is strong.

The diagonals should extend fully 11 inches beyond the back of the kite and a shorter distance (whatever the sticks will reach) to the front. When in place, mark plainly so you may set the kite up easily next time.

Frame the outer wings of the kite with string, and paper neatly. Glue the paper to the upright sticks and to the framing string, but not to the diagonals, unless you do not wish the kite to fold.

Tie the diagonals where they intersect, and attach a bridle loop 40 inches long at points A and B.

Figure 56 shows this kite complete. It is an excellent flier with great lifting power. Made according to directions, it has nearly 4,000 square inches of effective surface. Its rating is .83 ounce per square foot.

The name "Military Kite" is used since a number of nations have experimented with kites of this type for military observation work. It was reported that the Germans used such kites but of enormous size for sending observers aloft from their submarines. The correspondent giving this information indicated that cruising at a rate of 10 or 12 knots per hour would give the necessary "run" to lift a light man 150 feet or so in the air. He did not say how the observer got down or what happened if the string broke.

No. 24.   A Windmill Kite

Construct a Square Box Kite according to the directions given in No. 17 (p. 52). Prepare two sticks about ¼ by ⅜ by 26 inches and cross them diagonally through the bottom of the kite. Slit the ends. Run framing strings from the upper ends of the uprights through the slit in the long diagonals and to the lower end of the same uprights. This will give a triangular fin or buttress and will make the kite appear like a tapering windmill tower. Paper the fins, but do not glue the paper to the long diagonals unless you do not care to make the kite so it will fold. A roof may be formed with light sticks tied to the corners of the upper uprights, but it must not be completely papered. A cap of gilded paper gives the effect of a roof and is all that is necessary.

The windmill wheel may be made of light sticks with the blades set at an angle, but a simple wheel cut from a square

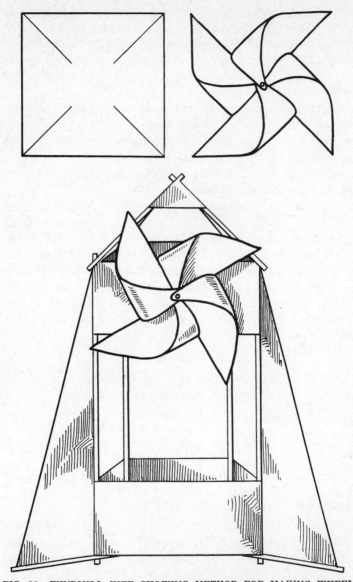

FIG. 57. WINDMILL KITE SHOWING METHOD FOR MAKING WHEEL

Attach the bridle far enough from the wheel so it will clear. An extra stick may be needed for the bridle attachment.

of stiff paper answers every need and is not so likely to get out of order. Make the wheel from a piece of heavy paper or light cardboard about 15 inches square in the manner shown in Figure 57, stiffening it with shavings glued in place as needed.

The axle or stick carrying the wheel should be about 14 inches long and should have a small knob at each end. A spool cut across will do for the knobs. Punch a small hole in the upper front surface of the kite and pass the axle through to a point corresponding to the hole on the surface of the opposite side. Put half a spool on the axle and secure it to the kite surface with glue. Do not glue the stick and spool together. Tie the axle to the intersection of the diagonals, reënforce the hole made in the front surface with a patch of cloth on the inside; glue the half spool (large side out) on the outer end of the axle and you are ready for the wheel.

Attach the wheel with a small nail. The nail should be first run through a button to form a washer, then carefully forced into the axle until the wheel is nearly tight.

The bridle loop will have to be quite long, say, 6 feet, and should be attached near the usual points of attachment for a box kite flown with one side to the wind.

The complete kite, made as above, rated .92 ounce per square foot. It was a good flier, but not as reliable as the other box kites.

Windmills are often used on kites to make certain parts move. Figure kites with moving eyes, automobile kites with revolving wheels, etc., are worked out on the same principle. Altering the design a little, and omitting the wheel, will make a lighthouse, and many other designs may be made with a little thought.

No. 25. A Cross Kite

Nearly all the square crosses, such as are used for lodge emblems, may be made by bowing the vertical member, leaving the horizontal member plane. Sometimes a keel on the back will have to be added. Should one of the slender crosses be desired, the box principle should be used. The more com-

FIG. 58. VARIOUS TYPES OF CROSSES THAT HAVE POSSIBILITIES IN KITE DESIGN
F is similar to E, except the ends are shaped as shown.

74

mon types of crosses are shown in Figure 58. Some of these
are used for religious and fraternal ceremonies, but others
are merely decorative designs and may be used where others
would not be appropriate. Consult an illustrated dictionary
for the names of these designs.

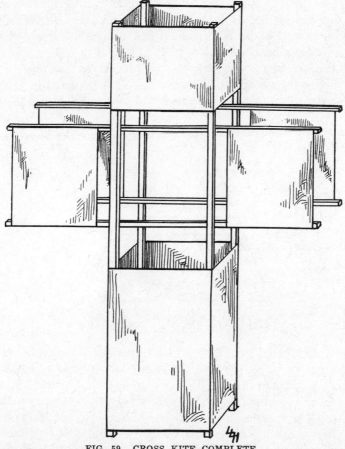

FIG. 59. CROSS KITE COMPLETE
The bridle will work well if attached to the uprights near the upper cross
stick. Notice the cross wings are not papered on top.

Styles A to F are built according to the method about to
be described. Most of the letters of the alphabet may be constructed in the same way and will fly fairly well with a little
special attention.

Prepare eight sticks ¼ by ⅜ by 26 inches. Lap the sticks 4 inches, glue and wrap, making four sticks 48 inches long. Using these as uprights, construct a rectangular box kite having a 12-inch face and a 6-inch depth. The top paper should be 10 inches and the bottom paper 20 inches wide.

The diagonal sticks should measure 13 inches from notch to notch, and should have the ends finished as described in Figure 39. The diagonals should rest on chips glued to the uprights as described in No. 17 (p. 52).

Prepare two sticks in the same manner as the uprights bringing their length to 36 inches. Lash one stick to the front upright, allowing an equal amount to project on each side of

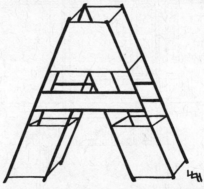

FIG. 60. SUGGESTION FOR A LETTER KITE BASED ON THE BOX-KITE AND CROSS-KITE PRINCIPLES

the kite. The stick should be fixed in position 12 inches from the top. The other stick should be similarly placed 12 inches farther down. Frame 10 inches of the ends of these sticks and paper neatly. Another pair of wings may be used on the back Cross Kite complete. One made by the author rated .90 ounce uprights, but it will be found that the additional pair contributes but little to the behavior or appearance of the kite.

The bridle should be attached to the intersections of the uprights and upper cross sticks. The style described is the single-arm Latin Cross, but others may be made on the same general plan.

The Latin Cross is very pretty when made of white crêpe paper and decorated with artificial snow, especially if flown at night and illuminated with an automobile spotlight. Such a flight is very appropriate at Easter. Figure 59 shows the cross kite complete. It rated .90 ounce per square foot of effective surface. It was a good flier.

Style B, Figure 58, may be used for Christmas Seal advertising, and Style H may be worked up for Red Cross drives.

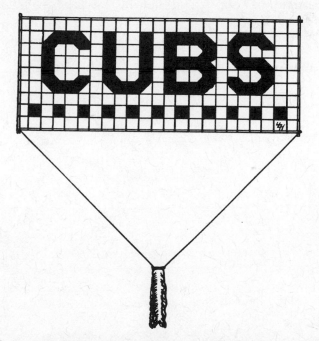

FIG. 61. SUGGESTION FOR A GROUP OF LETTERS TO BE PAPERED ON A FRAME AND FLOWN WITH A TAIL

The squares are 2 inches square and are made with light strings. Do not stretch the strings too tight. Dark blue or black mosquito netting is excellent for kites of this kind. Bridles are to be attached in the manner described under the Plane-Surface Kites (p. 11).

Of course, kites designed to make an appeal to the finer feelings of the spectators should be tried out carefully in private lest they dash down and spoil the effect they are supposed to make when flown in public.

Letters, if only a few are needed, may be made on the box principle. Figure 60 shows the plan for the letter A, but if the number of letters is considerable, they should be made flat, attached to a light frame and flown with a tail as in Figure 61.

The writer has made the twenty-five kites as varied in design as possible without using special tools or material. A number of styles have purposely been left out, such as birds, flies, centipedes, Mother Goose pictures, etc., since these may be planned and constructed with little trouble by anyone who can make a good box kite.

CHAPTER V

HINTS ON FLYING

WHERE TO FLY

It is easier to give instructions on where to fly than it is to find a suitable place. The ideal place is an open field or a place near a large body of water. Usually there are breezes or light winds in such places and troublesome obstructions are absent. Playgrounds and athletic parks in the larger cities provide room enough for ordinary flights, and it sometimes happens that the breeze aloft is sufficient to make high flying worth while. Often one finds an excellent breeze at the surface while a study of the smoke from the higher chimneys and stacks shows but little breeze aloft.

Winds whipping around corners and through streets are deceptive. It is well to study smoke and cloud movements before attempting very high flights in places of limited size.

Most cities have regulations against flying kites in the streets. A little thought will show us the wisdom of such a ruling. But, alas! so often the rule is winked at in one part of the city, and rigidly enforced in another that the temptation to fly or start the kite in the street is strong. The restriction on street flying was made, of course, for the protection of people in general. Formerly the safety of people driving horses was, probably, the reason for such rules. There is nothing that will more completely scare a horse out of his wits than a kite suddenly swooping in front of him or lashing him with its tail. A Japanese tells how a cavalry charge was broken up south of Yokohama many years ago, by flying kites in front of the enemy. Considering the scarcity of horses in that part of Japan, one is inclined to believe there was as much terror among the kite fliers as there was among the horses.

At present, danger arises from street flying from two sources—traffic and electric wires. The best plan is to play safe, and keep away from streets and lots where there is danger from traffic or contact with electric transmission lines.

Buildings are responsible for contrary currents of air, and these cause the kite to dart when the height of the building is reached. The result is usually a lost or broken kite.

There is more satisfaction in keeping your kites ready for use and going to a good place to fly, when the opportunity presents itself, than in trying to fly them in unsuitable places.

String

Many kinds of string are recommended for kite flying, but unless one is entering a tournament or preparing for some special kite event, no difficulty should be had in finding suitable string. The heaviest carpet and button thread are good for smaller kites, while common white carpet warp or a good grade of wrapping twine will serve for those herein described. Medium-laid 12-cord seine twine is the best for general flying, but it can be had only in pound hanks and is not often found in the smaller towns. It costs about a dollar a pound (1,600 feet). Good seine twine of this size will carry 10 pounds safely and will run 100 feet to the ounce. Twenty-four cord seine twine is strong enough for all but professional flying. If you are to use seine twine, be sure to get the medium laid. Soft laid does not stand the constant strain, and hard laid ravels too readily.

Some kitefliers wax their string. The string is not made stronger by the waxing, but, perhaps, it is made a little more durable and less liable to damage should it become wet. Waxing should be done carefully or difficulties will arise in winding and unwinding. The best way to wax a kite string is to let it run *lightly* over a piece of paraffin wax or candle a number of times instead of trying to wax it all at once. A very slight greasy feel to the clean hands is enough. This amount of waxing preserves the string, lessens the friction of the wind, and adds but little to the weight.

Linen shoe thread may be used as kite string if waxed, but I do not like it, since it is so sharp and firm that it is a punishment to handle it very long at a time even with a reel. Silk makes a wonderful kite string for a few minutes, but the fibers of silk slip past each other so easily that a continued pull soon causes the string to break.

Wire is sometimes mentioned by professional kite fliers. Without special equipment, wire is dangerous, even where there is no likelihood of getting tangled with electric circuits. The electrical condition of the atmosphere, even on clear days, is such that severe shocks may be given the flier if a wire line is used. I have received uncomfortable shocks by using a wet string and standing on an insulated stool; that is, I received the shock when I stepped off the stool. Should you desire to send up an aërial for radio work, keep the wire grounded until you are ready to connect it to your set. Then ground it before disconnecting and you will have no trouble. It is hoped that no one will be so foolish as to try to repeat Benjamin Franklin's experiment. The greatest marvel of his experiment is that he was not killed.

It must not be inferred that kite flying is dangerous. It is not. But discretion must be observed in using wires or electrical equipment.

WIND

In Chapter III, were explained some of the conditions contributing to flying that are not generally classed with winds. Upward and downward currents of air are hard to detect, since there is little evidence of such movements unless one is some distance from the ground. Any kite will be buoyed up to some extent by upward currents, and but few will remain aloft if a downward current is encountered.

Winds blowing parallel to the earth's surface are better for high or sustained flights than those that rise rapidly but make little progress otherwise. A study of smoke or cloud movements will give a great deal of information of value. In order to judge the direction of movement comfortably and correctly, level a mirror, face up, on the ground and mark the directions on it with bits of gummed paper. The reflections of the smoke and clouds in the mirror will move in the same compass direction that the smoke and clouds move in the sky. The mirror lessens the effect of perspective and allows the observer to take a more comfortable position than would be possible by looking into the sky. The mirror may be taken afield to watch the kite if one is obliged to fly the kite toward the sun.

While the kites described in this book will hardly reach above any but the lower clouds, still the study of cloud conditions is often helpful in choosing a good day to fly.

Some kites fly better in one wind than they do in another. A properly made elastic bridle will greatly increase the range of wind suitable for a given kite. As a rule, a kite darts when a strong gust of wind strikes it, since the movement is too sudden to swing much of the string with the kite, and a small circle is described. The elastic bridle allows the kite to lie flatter when the gust strikes it, and to utilize the extra force by leaping upward.

In the case of a tailed kite, one often finds that a kite will fly near the surface, but when aloft, it becomes "foxy" and requires more tail. If the kite is lowered and more tail added, difficulty is then had in raising the kite to its former height. The elastic bridle offsets this difficulty to a great extent, by allowing the kite to lie flatter so the tail will pull more nearly in line with the spine.

All other things being equal, the heavier of two kites will stand the stronger wind. This is due to a number of causes, among them being greater stiffness and the fact that more effort is required to move a heavy body than a light one.

For those who are fortunate enough to live near a large body of water, a word of caution may be in order about the failure of the wind. There is often an "on shore" breeze one time of the day, and an "off shore" breeze at another time. Between the two breezes, there is a period of calm which may be accompanied by downward currents. Sometimes the breeze blows one way during the day, and the other way at night. This change in direction is due to the different rates that land and water receive and radiate heat. It will be well to study the different times the breeze turns and to be careful not to have your kite out too far at the time. Sometimes there is a lull in the wind at the turning of the tide that will influence a kite.

A few years ago, I was interested in studying the origin of the trade winds along the west coast of South America. I used kites like No. 17, but a trifle larger than those described.

One evening after school I sent two kites aloft, and very soon the leader was lost among the clouds. A little later, the second kite was playing hide and seek in the clouds that drifted at about 1,000 feet. All at once, I noticed the second kite settling. I reeled in the string frantically but to no avail. The kite continued to sink. I then pulled in the string hand over hand, but the wind was gone and the cold air was drifting earthward. The leader dropped through the clouds and started toward the sea. The second kite was now within reach and bore every evidence of having been in a flurry of snow and frost. The sun dipped below the horizon and almost like a stone, the leader fell with several hundred feet of string. I recovered part of the string, but not the kite. I was wiser next time, and had my kites down before the off-shore wind failed.

I have had kites get into whirlwinds, and have seen them rise, fall, be drawn into the whirl, thrown out of the whirl, and torn to pieces. No two performances were the same. Lost and destroyed kites sometimes have scientific interest, but the boy or girl who has a good kite seldom cares to sacrifice it out of scientific curiosity. It is well, therefore, to choose a good place to fly, and to avoid freakish winds.

Flying

When you are ready to start a flight, make sure the bridle is in adjustment as called for in the directions. If the kite has been made recently, be sure it is dry. Knot the flying string to the tow string and stand with the back to the wind. When the wind pulls the kite strongly, toss the kite into the air and let out a little string. If the kite sinks, stop letting out the string until the kite gains some height, or run a few steps. If the kite darts suddenly, let out the string so it will come down easily. Do not drag the kite on the ground; go to the kite and try again. If the kite does not rise or if it continues to dart, it may need adjusting, or there may not be enough wind or there may be too much wind. If there is not enough wind, all that can be done is to wait for a better time. Sometimes running with the kite will get it up far enough to take advantage of a breeze that will carry it higher, but prolonged running has little to commend it; in addition to being tiresome, it has the further disadvantage that more than one person is required to start the flight.

Too much wind may be offset by using more tail in the case of the tailed kites, more bow in the bow kites and turning less of the surface of the box to the wind, or shifting the bridle of the box kites.

Sometimes a kite goes well for a time, but refuses to climb past a certain height. It may be that a strata or layer of calm is reached. If so, there is usually another breeze a little higher up moving in a different direction from that of the surface wind. Often the kite may be made to climb out of the calm by letting out a quantity of string and then giving a number of short pulls. In this case, the kite may continue to ascend after the upper wind is reached; the various layers of air and their movements are shown then by the directions taken by the different parts of the string.

Bear in mind that some kites are better fliers than others, even if made from the same directions. Small differences in size, rigidity, paper tension, weight, bow, and what not, all contribute to a kite's performance. Kites are described in this book as excellent, good, fair, and moderate fliers. Some moderate fliers like the Fisherman Kite, require considerable patience to adjust and fly successfully, but those having other ratings fly without difficulty. Patience, prudence, and practice will enable anyone to learn to fly a kite.

Adjustments

If the bridle intersection is too high, the kite will lie too flat, but will probably fly in a light breeze. If the intersection is too low, the kite becomes top-heavy and goes round and round or darts violently. Persistent darting to one side is probably due to the bridle being too short on that side. The towing point should be shifted accordingly. Sometimes a "foxy" kite may be improved by using a longer bridle; that is, by having the towing point farther from the kite.

Various ways of attaching bridles have been explained in the foregoing chapters, but conditions and methods of kite-making practiced by others may make changes necessary.

If it is necessary to alter the position of the towing point, do so cautiously an inch at a time. All the loops of the bridle must be changed if the alteration is very much. Adjust the vertical string from the top, and the horizontal strings from both sides making fast after each adjustment. If the towing string slips along the bridle, it may be kept in place with a drop of glue.

Darting may also be due to a lack of tail in the tailed kites or to a lack of bow in the bow kites. The necessary corrections are easily made. If the darting takes the form of rather large circles, causing the kite to gradually lose altitude, tighten the lower loop of the bridle a little without lowering the towing point. That is, equalize the pull on the upper and lower part of the bridle. Tailed kites usually ride at about 45 degrees from the vertical, the tail flowing away at a greater angle. Bow and box kites should lie flatter when flying. Box kites sometimes fly with the long sticks in a horizontal position and refuse to climb. In this case, fix a bridle to the kite so the towing point will lie at a distance from the kite equal to about half its height and about one fifth or one third the distance from the top. If the wind is strong, use one third; If very faint, try one fifth.

Too much tail causes a kite to rise slowly and to be sluggish in the air. Determine the least tail required and add a little, as the breeze may be fresher aloft and more tail will be needed. Too much bow lessens the lifting power of a bow kite and has a tendency to make the kite top-heavy. If the surfaces or cells of a box kite are too close together, the kite will be unsteady as will the tetrahedral kites if made with unbroken surfaces very much larger than the one described in this book.

Having acquired some knowledge of kites and flying, you are now in a position to plan and make stunt kites of various kinds.

Winding In

It is a good plan to allow more time for winding in than it takes to send the kite up. Without a reel, winding in becomes a task and takes away much of the kiteflier's fun and enthusiasm. It will be well to make a reel as soon as convenient if one expects to use more than a hundred yards of string at a time. Do not wind in the string too fast or the kite may dart. One or two plunges at a great height are nothing to worry about, but as the kite approaches the ground, difficulties begin to increase. To land a kite successfully near at hand requires some skill, and one should strive to attain at least a reasonable amount of it. There is no fun in finishing a successful flight with a disastrous landing.

When the kite has been brought down successfully, it should be detached from the flying string. If it is a bow or box kite, it should be folded and made into a secure package. Tailed kites should have their tails rolled up neatly and put into a paper sack kept for the purpose. Tails so kept do not get tangled easily and are easily carried about.

Store the kites in a safe dry place away from mice and rats. These animals and cockroaches are very fond of a paper and paste combination. Highly colored kites should be kept out of strong light. Take care of your kites. While the actual cost of materials is small, the labor required to make them gives them a value worthy of the best of care.

CHAPTER VI

KITE ACCESSORIES

A REEL

One may make a kite and fly it at moderate heights with no other equipment than a stick on which to wind the string, but many of the kites described in this book fly so well that

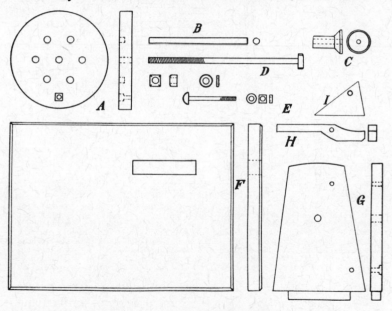

FIG. 62. PARTS OF A KITE REEL

A, disc forming ends of reel, ¾ by 5½ inches—two required; B, rod forming drum part of reel, ⅜ by 5½ inches—six required; C, spool cut as shown, for handle—one required; D, flat-head (machine) bolt, ⅜ by 8-inch, washers and nuts as described—one required; E, round-head stove bolt as described— two required; F, base, ¾ by 9 by 12 inches, with hole to receive upright—one required. The hole should be on the lower side of the drawing for left-handed kite fliers; G, upright cut from 5 by 8-inch piece as shown—one required. The lower hole is for the brake bolt, the center hole for the axle, and the upper hole should be opposite the hole in the disc. A nail may then be slipped through the upright and the disc thus locking the reel; H is the brake. Shape to fit—one required; I is a block of sufficient thickness to place the brake in line with the inner disc of the drum—one required.

the boy or girl making them will find much enjoyment in high and decorative flying.

Winding in great lengths of string becomes very tiresome, and often difficulty is encountered in winding the string so it will wind out easily the next time and yet be free from tangles. A reel solves the difficulties, and a good reel is so easily made that nobody need be without one. The only tools

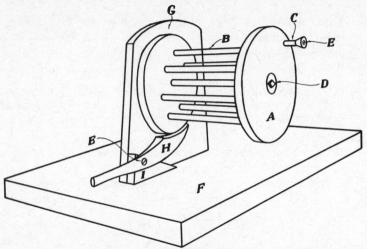

FIG. 63. THE REEL SET UP.

See the description for cautions about the bolt bearing the handle. The axle D is assembled as follows: Head of bolt, washer, reel drum, washer, nut, washer, upright, washer, nut, nut. The bolt carrying the brake is assembled as follows: Head of bolt, washer, brake block, nut set in the upright, the upright, washer, nut, nut. The block should be nailed lightly to the upright, and the upright should be glued and nailed in the base. Be sure to allow plenty of play between the drum and the axle, as the string will shrink at times and cause the reel to clamp fast to the axle. Letters same as in Fig. 62.

needed in making a reel that are not listed in Chapter I are a brace and two bits. The bits should be ⅜ of an inch and ¼ of an inch respectively. The materials required are as follows:

One ⅜ by 8-inch machine bolt with threads cut full one fourth the length with four washers and three nuts.

Two ¼ by 3-inch stove bolts with three washers and two nuts to each bolt.

One large spool for the reel handle.

One large nail or spike.

A ⅜-inch dowel rod, 3 feet long makes excellent rods for the reel drum, but the rods may be planed or whittled to about the right size and finished by driving through a machine nut. Be sure they are not less than ⅜ of an inch in diameter. The lumber and nails may be obtained from the ends and partition of the orange crate. The drawings in Figures 62 and 63 describe the making of the reel step by step, so only a few cautions need be given in the text.

If you are left-handed, turn the base over so the hole for the upright will be to your right when the longer part of the base is toward you.

The hole for the crankbolt should be first countersunk on the inside of the disc with a ⅜-inch bit just deep enough to allow a washer and one nut to lie in it when screwed up tight. Bore the hole through the rest of the way with the ¼-inch bit. The bolt must not be screwed in past the nut, lest the string catch on it and be cut by the sharp edge. A good plan is to glue a heavy piece of paper over this attachment before the string is wound on.

The block carrying the brake is countersunk in the same manner on the side that fits against the upright piece. The brake is a little troublesome to fit, so it is a good plan to fit it in place first, using a small nail as the pivot, then following the nail hole with the bits.

Do not bore the holes for the rods clear through. Bore until the nib of the bit can be seen, then turn back and clean out the hole. Try to have the holes all the same depth, holding the bit perpendicular to the surface when you bore, and taking care that you do not unexpectedly burst through the board.

The moving parts should fit snugly but should not bind or catch. Damp weather and tight winding make the reel hard to turn, but storing in a dry place usually is all that is necessary to loosen it again.

There are many kinds of reels, some of them elaborate affairs, but for all ordinary flying, the one described here answers every need.

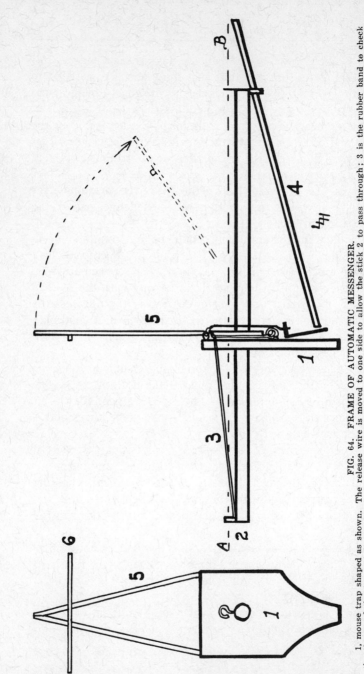

FIG. 64. FRAME OF AUTOMATIC MESSENGER.

1, mouse trap shaped as shown. The release wire is moved to one side to allow the stick 2 to pass through; 3 is the rubber band to check the throw of the trap; 4 is the bowsprit that trips the trap throwing the mast; 5 is forward as shown by the dotted line. The sail is attached to the double mast and the yard arm 6. The kite string is shown at AB. The kite is beyond B.

MESSENGERS

The simplest messenger is a piece of paper having a hole near the center and a slit so it may be pinned around the string. These go only toward the kite, and after a number have been sent up, interfere with the flying. The trick of getting the messenger to return has been described in many magazine articles; in almost every case, it depends on folding the sail at the right time so the messenger glides back under the force of gravity. The messenger shown in Figure 64 does not fold the sail, but sets it at an angle so that the wind aids in sending the messenger back to the flier. Various releases have been devised, but I do not think any as simple and as positive as the one here described. A yacht is the usual form of messenger, although I have seen a messenger shaped like a mouse run up the kite string to be later overtaken and brought back by one shaped like a cat. But fancy messengers call for good flying conditions, and too much disappointment should not accompany their failure to perform.

If a yacht messenger is to be used, make the hull of thin cardboard, fitted to blocks of thin light wood. The center block is a spring mousetrap, spring toward the prow, bait treadle down. The jaw is prevented from going too far forward by a check made of a strong rubber band and a string. Two light sticks are fitted to the sides of the jaw for a mast, and to the mast is rigged a sail. Parchment paper or tracing cloth makes a good sail. The bowsprit passes through the stem of the vessel and makes contact with the treadle of the trap. The trip on the string may be almost anything that is large enough to do the trick without adding unnecessary weight to the system. A small ring or even a short stick serves very well. The trip should be placed some distance from the kite, about the place where the string curves sharply upward.

The yacht is hung to the kite line by means of little screw eyes that have been spread a trifle so the string may pass into them without having to be cut and threaded through. A hole will have to be made in the trap to allow the string to pass. The whole scheme is to have the sail erect when the messenger is climbing, and when the trap is thrown, to have the sail swing forward parallel to the string. Both gravity and the wind will aid in returning the messenger to the flier.

No dimensions are given, since the style of vessel is one of individual choice. The author has one that is 12 inches long and weighs 3 ounces. In a stiff breeze it works very well.

PARACHUTES

To make a parachute, roll a cone of tissue paper about 10 inches in diameter and 8 inches deep. When nicely shaped, paste it together and let it dry. The shape and size may be obtained by cutting out a circle of paper 14 inches in diameter and then cutting out a piece like a fourth of a pie and pasting the edges of the cut together. When dry, crumple the paper until soft and glue 4 threads about 2 feet long at equal distances around the base of the cone. Holding the cone by the tip, even the threads and knot together. Experiment a little to find a pebble that will make the parachute open and sail when dropped from a short distance. The pebble may be attached to the threads by wrapping it in a tuft of cloth or crêpe paper.

A parachute may be made over a crock or mixing bowl, and if you care to take the trouble, one may be built up with a number of sections cut like those of an umbrella. Do not use too much paste or glue or the parachute will be too stiff to open.

The most satisfactory attachment is a combination attachment and release.

TIME RELEASE

Stir a spoonful of gunpowder or saltpeter in a few spoonfuls of water. When dissolved, stir in a quantity of common string. Let the string become thoroughly soaked and then hang it in loops to dry. The string is now a slow fuse. Cut off a piece, and determine roughly its rate of burning. Usually, it will burn from 1 to 2 inches per minute, so a few inches is sufficient for each release. Tie a thread to the parachute loop, and suspend the parachute a few inches from the kite. In case of kite No. 10, suspend from the lower cross stick. Then tie a piece of fuse string to the thread, or run the thread through the fuse with a needle. When everything is ready, light the tip of the fuse and put up the kite. A parachute on each side is better than one, as the kite is more easily balanced.

Fuses are also used for releasing camera shutters in making aërial photographs, for opening boxes aloft, and for setting off fireworks high in the air. Firecrackers, punk, and cigarettes have been used for fuses, but the manufactured fuse works better, unless a signal is needed at a given time as described in the paragraph on photography (p. 95).

A Confetti Shower

Secure a small pasteboard box that has a loose overlapping lid. Attach the lid at one end by means of a paper hinge. Sew a loop of fuse through the end so the lid will be released when the fuse burns away. The box is to hang to the kite string, lid down, and hinge next to the flier. A longer fuse should be tied around the thread fastening the box to the line, but care must be taken lest the kite line get afire. Put a handful of confetti, chopped paper, bran, chaff, or maple seeds in the box, attach to the kite line, light both fuses and send aloft. Do not allow too much fuse as there is a limit to the time a box will remain flying in the air without interfering with the flight of the kite. Some fliers prefer to fix the box to the string, and reel in for another charge.

A box 200 feet above the ground gives a wonderful effect; even at a less height the experiment is very pretty and well worth the time and effort.

Decorations

Bear in mind that the tail of a kite is for a definite purpose, so do not burden it with unnecessary decorations. Carry your banners and flags on the kite line some distance from the kite. A banner should be hung in the proper position, and the top should be hung straight. By top, is meant the part of the banner that *is* the top when the banner is in the proper position to be read or examined. Fasten a light stick to this margin of the banner and hang it on the kite line so it will be horizontal when the height is reached where the banner is to fly. A trial or two may be necessary in order to secure the proper adjustment.

A national flag should fly horizontally, with the stick fastened to the margin of the flag that goes next to the mast or staff. Have the stick a trifle longer than the width of the flag and hang the stick vertically from the kite line with a guy cord tied to the bottom of the stick and to the kite line so the proper position will be kept. Be sure the flag flies right side up. Flying a flag upside down is a signal of distress and should be done only in time of dire need. Do not fly any flag or banner above any national flag. Only the chaplain's pennant is permitted to fly above the United States flag, and that only under certain conditions. Other flags not of national character, banners, or pennants may be flown lower on the kite line. Pennants are usually attached directly to the line. Streamers may be fixed to the kite line to suit. It is well not to overdo the decoration of a kite. Put up more kites rather than load a given kite or team of kites too much.

KITES IN TANDEM AND TEAMS

Kites for team flying should be tried out singly since a lazy kite will offset a good one with the result that the weight of both will hang on the line.

"He has too many kites on one string," is a saying equivalent to "too many irons in the fire" and is often heard, especially from older people. It is possible to have too many kites on one string, but three or four may be managed nicely with only a few precautions. Fly the first one about 200 feet, and the second one about half that distance on another string. Then tie the two strings securely to a small ring, cast-iron preferred, since a wire ring may open and release the kites.

A heavier string should be attached, the two flown about 200 feet, another ring added into which the third kite should be tied. It should be flying about 100 feet before it is tied in. Put up the second kite behind the leader, the third kite behind the team, etc., to avoid getting tangled. Decorations should be attached to the same ring as one of the kites. Only two sizes of string are necessary for kites like the ones here described.

PHOTOGRAPHY FROM KITES

First of all, use an inexpensive camera or kodak until you are sure that no disaster is likely to occur. Even then, a parachute a yard square attached to the handle and folded neatly so it will open in the event of a fall, may be a wise precaution.

Arrange a rubber band so it will jerk the shutter across or release it according to the make of camera. Then relieve the shutter from the pull of the rubber by a string to which is attached a fuse. Experiment with the release until you hit upon a plan that will work. Stubborn cases may be solved by using a firecracker with a long fuse made as described, and the release string running through the firecracker. Or, use a cartridge made by taking a few turns of wrapping paper around a pencil and glued so a shell is formed open at one end. Into this, place half a teaspoonful of black powder, insert the fuse deep into the powder, glue up the open end and run the shutter string through the body of the cartridge. A puff of smoke tells one when the shutter has been snapped. It may be necessary to rig the shutter control to a light stick.

Observe the rules necessary for making a good picture at the surface, such as focus for folding cameras, direction of light, pointing, changing the film, etc., and do not take it too much to heart if you fail the first few times. There is a knack in taking pictures from kites that must be mastered before one can be sure of success.

If you do not care to use a firecracker or cartridge, you may time the fuse, allowing plenty of time extra for it to work. Or, you may tie a tuft of paper to the fuse so it will be released a minute after the shutter. It will drift down slowly, and may be spied even if it is not seen the moment of its release.

A number of articles have been published on using a camera obscura, or dark box with a lens at one end and waxed paper at the other, to catch views of the country visible from the kite but not visible to the flier. The articles seem to be copied from a foreign writer who suggested that the picture focused on the waxed paper be examined by a telescope. Ask any photographer what he thinks about it and you will be convinced of its absurdity. A mirror might work if the angle made with the observer could be preserved, but the range of vision with such an aërial periscope is too limited to interest us. It is better to use photography and to take a chance of getting what we want in the picture.

For warrior kites, kite battles, etc., the reader is referred to books that deal with kite tournaments.

CHAPTER VII

USEFUL INFORMATION

Many things will occur to the amateur kitemaker that will be worth writing down for future use. In this chapter are given a few useful recipes and directions.

PASTE

A good paste may be made of flour. Sift a heaping tablespoonful of flour into a cup of lukewarm water. Beat thoroughly in order to remove all lumps. Add a scant teaspoonful of sugar and pour into a saucepan or other convenient utensil. Into the flour mixture pour a cup of vigorously boiling water stirring constantly. Keep at a boiling temperature, and stir until the color becomes opalescent. Then stir in a half teaspoonful of ground cloves or cinnamon and transfer to a jar or can. Let the paste cool before using, thinning if necessary with warm water.

The manufacturers of minute tapioca describe a paste that is unsurpassed: One cup boiling water; 2 level tablespoonfuls minute tapioca; 3 level tablespoonfuls sugar; 1 teaspoonful lemon juice; 1 pinch salt; 1 large pinch cinnamon.

Stir the ingredients into the boiling water and cook in a double boiler until very thick. A little salt added to the water in the outer vessel raises the boiling point and lessens the time required for cooking. Let the paste cool before using. Keep covered when not in use, and the paste will keep a long time.

GLUE

Various kinds of liquid glue are to be had, the standard brands being very satisfactory. Prepared glue is costly, but only a little is required. Too much glue is almost as bad as none at all. When gluing kite sticks, a thin even coat on clean, dry wood is much better than a heavy daub on a damp or dirty stick. After gluing, the sticks should be held together with a clamp or by wrapping with string, but the sticks should not be clamped too tightly or they may break at the joint.

Liquid glue should be thinned with warm water when it is to be used on paper. The regular strength is thicker than need be, and it adds extra weight.

If you prefer to make your own glue, select clean sticks or flakes of glue and beat them into fine pieces. This may be

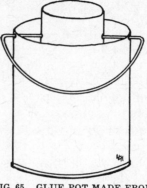

FIG. 65. GLUE POT MADE FROM
TWO EMPTY CANS AND A
PIECE OF WIRE.
The inner can is kept above the
outer can to prevent burning the
glue.

done by putting the glue into a cloth, covering the cloth with several thicknesses of newspaper and breaking with a hammer. Avoid ground glue, since much of the stuff sold for glue is really calciminers' sizing and is unfit for joining. After the glue is beaten to bits, select one large and one small tin can, beat down the rough edges, and wash the cans carefully. Punch two holes opposite each other near the top of the large can and two holes opposite each other about an inch from the top of the smaller can. Arrange a bail as shown in Figure 65. A cheap brush completes the outfit.

Place about an inch of broken glue in the inner can and cover with cold water. Let it stand several hours in a moderately warm room. Then fill the outer can half full of clean water and heat to just below the boiling point until the glue in the inner can melts. The glue is then ready for use, and should be applied hot. Do not boil vigorously lest the pot boil over. Do not leave the brush in the glue, but clean it out when you have finished using it. The water in the outer can must be kept clean, so it should be drained out and the glue outfit put in a clean, dry place when not in use.

It is a good plan to make up only a small amount of glue at a time, since mixed glue decomposes rapidly in warm weather. If care is taken to keep the remaining glue in a cool dry place, it may be reheated and used without special attention. If the glue is dry, a little water will have to be added before heating, but if the glue is gummy, or gives easily under the pressure of a stick, try reheating without adding water.

BUILT-UP STICKS

In making large kites, it often happens that no suitable sticks may be had. One must either have the sticks planed out of heavier stock, or build up a stick or sticks from light material. I prefer the built-up stick, since the extra material

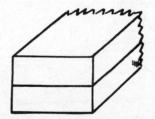

PLAIN LAP FOR A BUILT-UP
STICK
Not so desirable as Fig. 67.

may be put where it is needed. If we make a kite stick by gluing sticks together as shown in Figure 66, and another like that shown in Figure 67, the latter will be the more satisfactory. The rib may be flared out to secure the advantage of a flat stick at intersections. The principal part of the stick and the rib should be made separately, gluing together after they are dry and strong. Where more than one stick of a kind is required, they should be made from the same kind of material, the identical parts being cut from the same board or one nearly like it. Sticks of unequal weight, stiffness, and tendency to warp will result if built-up sticks

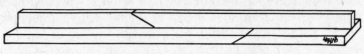

FIG. 67. A BUILT-UP STICK
Notice the joints of the two members do not lie directly over each other.

are made in a haphazard way. A stick built up from orange-crate boards, and shaped like the one shown in Figure 67, will be found very satisfactory for all-round work. To make such a stick, proceed as follows:

Select two or three boards having a straight edge grain showing both white and pink wood. Cut sticks enough from the pink side of the boards to give sufficient length when lapped about three inches. Mark the board so you can tell one side from the other, and so you can keep the grain running in the same direction. Keep the same side of the strips uppermost when joining. Split out the sticks rather than cut them out, allowing plenty of width for final dressing and bringing to size. Mark and cut as shown in Figure 68.

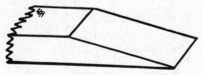

FIG. 68. STICK CUT FOR LAPPING

A little practice with a sharp knife will enable you to cut the bevels for the joint with a single stroke. A plane may be used if needed. Lay the sticks out on a solid board placing a paper under the joints so the glue will not stick them fast to the board. Line them up carefully and glue firmly together by applying hot glue and nailing a block over the joint taking care that the nails do not injure the stick. Clamps may be used if obtainable.

Build up another stick in the same manner, using the white part of the wood.

Allow the two members to dry 24 hours in a warm, dry room, then carefully remove the blocks.

Plane each member down to the desired width, using a tight string or a straight board to gauge their straightness. Finish the flat edges with very light planing. Use the pink stick for the principal part and the white stick for the rib. The joints or the two members should not come directly together, but should be at least five inches apart.

Having shaped the rib to suit, blocks should be prepared so the two members may be clamped every four inches. Apply hot glue and block or clamp without delay. Wipe off the excess glue and let dry at least 24 hours before using. Sandpaper lightly, using a block of wood with the sandpaper bent over the corner so you may get into the angle between the two members. If a flare of the rib is desired, it should be added last and wrapped in place with string. A light coat of shellac or varnish keeps out moisture and preserves the wood.

Sometimes a little glue or a shaving glued in place will stiffen a flimsy stick or will correct a built-up stick that will not behave like the others.

Larger Kites

You will not have great success in making very large kites without special materials, although a kite two or three times the size of the ones described herein can be made with a little care using built-up sticks made from orange-crate boards. Suppose one wishes to make a two-stick kite without making numerous joints in the sticks. A little calculation will show that a kite $2\frac{1}{2}$ times as large each way may be made with very little more effort than one twice as large, while a kite three times as large will require an extra splice in the sticks. Multiplying each dimension by $2\frac{1}{2}$, we have, length 65 inches, width 55 inches. If the weight goes above $3\frac{1}{2}$ ounces, we are losing flying performance for the sake of size.

Since the kite will be but very little thicker than the small one from which it is copied, the sticks need not be made 1 by $\frac{3}{4}$ inch as one might at first think. Using boards of the thickness of orange-crate material, a built-up stick $\frac{3}{4}$ inch wide for the principal member and with a rib $\frac{1}{2}$ inch high will be found ample. The cross stick may be made a little lighter. Lay the flat sides of the sticks together, the spine next to the paper; frame and paper as usual.

Thin paper will have to be reënforced in large kites. The gummed paper tape used for sealing boxes and packages is excellent for reënforcing. Small amounts may often be had from merchants for a few cents. If the tape is not easy to obtain, cut strips of heavy paper 2 inches wide and long enough to reach a few inches beyond the kite in each direction. Paste evenly, transfer to a clean table, pasted side up, and butt the thin paper together on the pasted strip. Let the paper dry before moving. String dipped in glue and laid across the crêpe of crêpe paper makes a good reënforcement. The paper must first be drawn to the tension desired and objectionable wrinkles removed.

For a large kite, it is better to use a wide tail rather than to increase the length of the tail. Four-inch festoon may be had, which if increased by a narrow festoon on each side, brings the width of the tail to seven inches. The area of the two-stick kite described in Chapter I is 268 square inches and the area of the tail is $1\frac{1}{2} \times 15 \times 12 = 270$ square inches. The area of a festoon tail should be about the area of the kite. Then for a 7-inch tail, a little figuring will give the proper length. Area of kite inside the framing string $= \frac{1}{2}$ of 64×54 inches $= 1,728$ square inches. The tail should be 1,728 divided by $7 = 247$ inches long which is a bit under 21 feet. Of course, other kinds of tails will have to be worked out by experiment.

TAILS

While paper festooning is recommended for tails, it is not always at hand. A piece of paper folded a number of times into long pleats and cut here and there with the scissors as our grandmothers used to cut shelf paper gives a light fancy design that offers considerable resistance to the air. A string should be glued down the center line and bits of gay colored paper pasted along the edge. When dry, the tail may be shaped up with the scissors.

Many kitemakers cling to the string tail with twists of paper tied in at regular intervals, with a bright-colored cloth at the end. There is no objection to such a tail, if it is kept fluffy, but if hurriedly made, it is likely to be heavy and stiff in its motion.

Suggestions have been given for special tails, such as the string of fish for the Fisherman, the skipping rope for the Girl, and the ladder for the Balloon. In the case of the Imp, the kite was made to serve the tail instead of the tail to serve the kite. Since imps are supposed to have tails, the tail was made and the appropriate figure attached.

A comet kite made with a five-point or six-point star as a head and with appropriate streamers for a tail should not be difficult to construct, and should have great possibilities for decoration.

If one can get the round festooning, a little color, a little trimming, and a little patience will develop an excellent tail shaped like a snake. Change the lines of the Frog Kite a trifle and add a limber tail and an alligator may be had with little trouble. The tail of a kite is not a nuisance—it is a possibility.

To Find the Altitude of a Kite

It is not an easy matter to find the altitude at which a kite flies. A little thought will make it clear that neither the angle at which a kite flies nor the amount of string used will determine the height. In fact, one cannot always determine the height of ascent by knowing both the amount of string and the angle since lateral currents and unequal strata of air do not allow the string to follow any regular curve.

All observations to give correct results must be made from two positions or stations a known distance apart. If the angles at which the kite flies and the distance the stations are apart are known, the altitude may be computed by special methods. But the easiest way is by using what may be called a "clinograph." You can make one easily as follows:

Select one of the end boards of an orange crate, and either rule it into squares or paste a sheet of squared paper on it. Half-inch squares will answer very well. Drive a row of brads along the right-hand edge, putting one brad in each square as shown in Figures 69 and 70. Select a piece of

braided fishline 3 feet long and tie the middle to the brad in
the upper right-hand corner. Attach iron nuts or other small
heavy objects to each end of the string. Let one string and
nut hang outside the brads, and the other inside just clearing
the board. To make an observation, let the strings hang free
as plumb lines. Sight along the top edge of the board, AB,

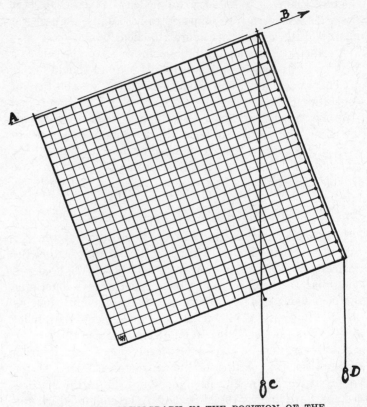

FIG. 69. THE CLINOGRAPH IN THE POSITION OF THE
FIRST OBSERVATION
Sight along AB to the kite, with a plumb bob C free to find a vertical
position.   Secure the line with a pin or tack.   Plumb bob D remains
outside the row of brads as described in the text.

to the kite. When the plumb line nearest you finds its position, secure it taut along the face of the board by means of
a tack. Without moving the kite, walk directly toward it for
some distance, say 150 feet, and swing the other plumb line

under the fifteenth brad from the top (that is, the sixteenth brad in the row) and observe as before. The intersection of the two strings will indicate on the board the altitude the kite is flying. You will note that the squares in this case are taken as 10 feet, since you allowed 15 squares for the 150-foot line between the observations. Then if the strings intersect or

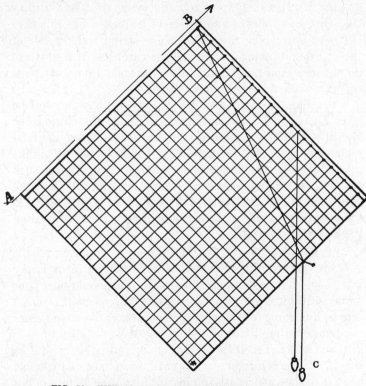

FIG. 70.   THE CLINOGRAPH AT THE END OF THE
SECOND OBSERVATION

The plumb C is held in place while the plumb D is released as described in the text. The squares in this case are considered as being ten
feet square.   The plumb lines intersect at a point between the eighth
and ninth square from the row of brads.   The distance represented is
therefore nearly 85 feet which represents the height the kite is above
the observer.   That would be about 90 feet from the ground.   The
squares may be given any value desired.   In this case, if the squares
are taken as 25 feet, the fifteenth square (sixteenth brad) would represent a base line of 375 feet, and the intersection would read off
8½×25=212.5 feet, plus the height of the observer, (say 4.5 feet)
giving 217 feet for the altitude of the kite.   Do not be dissappointed
in this device.   Kite altitudes are nearly always overestimated.   When
a great deal of string is used, a single kite is seldom higher than a
fifth of the length of the string.

cross at 8½ squares to the left of the line of brads, the kite is flying at an altitude of 85 feet.

There are two sources of error; namely, imperfections of the instrument, and imperfections in the observations. Since the plumb lines do not form their angles from the same brad, a slight error creeps into the plotting but the error cannot be greater than the distance the brads are apart. The width of the strings also makes another error probable, but this may be offset by reading the right of one string and the left of the other, and taking an average. Be careful that the strings do not scrape on the board and that the wind does not blow the nuts while making an observation.

The ground between the observation stations may not be level. One should avoid broken country for observations, or else allow for the difference in the altitudes when the final plotting is made. A clinograph may have adjustments to take care of these errors, but a little judgment will correct such errors as are likely to arise. Figures 69 and 70 show the clinograph in the positions of the two observations and also the method for reading the altitude of the kite directly from the plotted readings.

RECORDS

Keep a record of your kites and how they perform. Every kite should have a distinguishing mark and should bear your name and address on the frame. Almost anyone will return a kite or kiteframe to its owner. Select a blank book and enter the name, rating, dates of flying, and flying ability of each kite you make. Tell its good points, its bad points, and how the latter were corrected. You will soon have a valuable handbook that will assist you in building almost any kind of kite desired.

BIBLIOGRAPHY

MILLER, C. M. *Construction and Flying of Kites.* Manual Arts Press, Peoria, Ill.

MILLER, C. M. *Kitecraft and Kite Tournaments.* Manual Arts Press, Peoria, Ill.

INDEX